D1057968

Treading Softly

Treading Softly

Paths to Ecological Order

Thomas Princen

The MIT Press
Cambridge, Massachusetts
London, England

For information about special quantity discounts, please email special_sales@mitpress.mit.edu

This book was set in Sabon by MIT Press. Printed and bound in the United States of America.

Library of Congress Cataloging-in-Publication Data

Princen, Thomas, 1951–
Treading softly : paths to ecological order / Thomas Princen.
    p.   cm.
Includes bibliographical references and index.
ISBN 978-0-262-01417-5 (hardcover : alk. paper) 1. Human ecology—Economic aspects. 2. Nature—Effect of human beings on. 3. Consumption (Economics)—Environmental aspects. 4. Sustainable development. 5. Environmental policy. I. Title.
GF41.P73 2010
304.2—dc22
                                                            2009034032

10 9 8 7 6 5 4 3 2 1

Contents

Preface   vii
Acknowledgments   xiii

1   Within Our Means   1

I   The Disordered Order   19

2   From House to Home: A Parable   21
3   To the Heart of the Beast   29
4   Only When . . .   49

II   A Home Economy   59

5   Principles   61
6   The Elm Stand   79
7   Beyond the Consumer Economy   91

III   Tools for an Ecological Order   103

8   It Isn't Easy   105
9   Work, Workers, and Working: Toward an Economy That
    Works   119

10 Speaking of the Environment: Two Worlds, Two
    Languages   135

11 To Sustainabilize: The Adaptive Strategy of World-
    views   157

12 The New Normal   179

Notes   197
Index   207

Preface

In an essay on water in his classic book *Desert Solitaire*, Edward Abbey poses a question: Is there a shortage of water in the desert? No, he says, there's no shortage of water in the desert. There's just the right amount.[1]

For a long time, the wisdom in such an observation could be ignored. A great nation had to be built, an industrial economy created, foes of democracy defeated. Resources—timber, minerals, oil, water, soil—were virtually unlimited, and waste sinks—where the residues and runoff and combustion gases went—an alien concept.

That time is over. What was perfectly normal in the past—harvesting a resource until it was depleted, then moving on—is fast becoming abnormal. What were once strictly local environmental problems now quickly bump up against global constraints. Yesterday's living well is today's living well beyond our means.

Imagine, though, if back then the building of a great nation and the creation of a dynamic, growing economy had to be conducted so as to fit a resource-constrained continent, indeed, a resource-constrained planet. Or imagine that the early settlers actually arrived on a small island, more were coming, and there was no going back. In either situation, the economy would have to be supremely sensitive to excess—excess extraction, excess consumption, excess waste. They certainly could strive for a better life, they could experiment and solve problems, but they couldn't strive for more and more stuff. Rather, they would have to strive to live within their means, including the regenerative means of forests and grasslands and fisheries and water supplies.

With a history of seemingly endless resources and innocuous waste deposition and great economic wealth, imagining such scenarios is difficult today. But not impossible. This book aims to spur similar thought experiments precisely because we have no choice but to actually live within our means. It is time to build a material system of resource flows, what we might call an "economy," that operates as if we have just the right amount of resources. The goal, then, would be to live well by living well within the capacities of those resources.

Images

So this book creates images of the possible. All too often, I find in my experience as researcher and teacher and citizen, people discover that the planet is in serious jeopardy and that life as we know it, especially in the affluent North, will be changing, and changing dramatically. They strain to see into that future. Yet all they see are (1) extensions of the present, only greened up and made more efficient; or (2) collapse scenarios, courtesy of Hollywood, gloom-and-doom scientists, environmentalists, and some prominent writers.

The problem is not that these images are entirely unrealistic or lack hope. Rather, they are not imaginative. The proponents of techno-green apparently only see the superficial overlay of modern life, its cars and buildings and parks, its commodity exchanges and energy supply networks, which are contributing to the problem and will have to be improved. Similarly, the gloom-and-doomers can only see the present minus a whole lot of energy and material. Since the only knowledge we have of such an existence, indeed, of such deprivation, is from the past, presumably a dark and miserable past, then collapse is sure to be, well, dark and miserable.

These images are certainly compelling. But they are not helpful, let alone hopeful, and most important, once again, not imaginative. Their proponents seem unable to imagine that humans, for all their frailties and abominations, tend to rise to the occasion. When challenged, they cope and they adapt. And they do not much appreciate autocrats and technocrats solving their problems for them. In fact, my long-standing view, one at least as plausible and as well substantiated as the views of the techno-greens and the gloom-and-doomers, is that humans are at their best when

1. they help themselves and help others;
2. they are productive, creative, and self-directed;
3. they have problems to solve.

Or, as my colleague Ray De Young reminds me, humans are not well adapted to affluence. We may go for the conveniences and comforts. But we are designed to explore and experiment and solve problems, and to occasionally struggle, and to do so mostly with others, as a clan or a team or a community. However, we are *not* well designed to deal with continuous abundance, including cheap food, cheap drugs, cheap water, and cheap oil.

So in this book I offer a "third view," one that is, I claim, positive, though fundamentally different from contemporary, mainstream views. Some of the images in this view are conveyed by *stories*—vignettes, anecdotes, histories, case studies, even a parable and a fanciful dialogue. Others are conveyed by ideas, concepts, words—in short, *language*, the bread and butter of a social theorist. My position (and that of countless philosophers, linguists, critical theorists, historians, anthropologists, sociologists, and many others) is that it is through language that we *see* and *construct* our world. The scientific, industrial, and financial trends all point to a new world; for that we need a new worldview and new language. So I ask you the reader to bear with me on this academic score. This is not an academic treatise, but it does spew out terms, what I like to think of as *nominations* for that worldview and that language.

This work, then, is intended to be both more helpful and more hopeful than the green-it-up-and-keep-it-all-going view and the gloom-and-doom-woe-is-us view. I will have more to say about hope at the end. Meanwhile, I urge you readers to do a bit of exploring and re-visioning yourselves, in these pages (though certainly not every chapter will be helpful) and in your daily lives, however big or small. See if you can find the new in the familiar, the stories and the words that help us all innovate and solve problems and adapt. See if you can do good work, however hard it may be, without an endless stream of goods coming from afar.

Tough Questions

In my graduate class on sustainability, students often grill me (though I keep telling them I am supposed to be grilling them!). They ask hard questions like, If we consume less, won't it hurt the economy? Or, how can we really do things sustainably when our leaders don't have the political will to act? Or, what we really need are sustainable technologies, more efficient ways of using resources, right? And so on. One year, a student with considerable business experience, Mark Rabinsky, was particularly annoying. He just kept asking such questions, and re-asking them. I'd declare dire trends and he'd express his skepticism. I'd raise my eyebrows and he'd remind me of the power of markets and technology. Trying to be the ever-patient and responsive teacher, I'd answer his questions—not always effectively, I'm sure.

But at one point my exasperation must have come through. Mark said, "I'm sorry to keep asking you these questions. I'm trying not to be obnoxious. But these are the questions I get. And I don't have good answers." Others in the class nodded. They too, I discovered, were looking for responses to well-worn questions and claims and assertions. They were already well versed in the environmental facts and the need to act. Their biggest problem, on a day-to-day basis, with fellow students and relatives and employers, was answering these tough questions.

So, much of what follows are answers for Mark and countless other students and readers and editors and audience members. These answers hopefully act as two-headed hammers, one head to knock down assumptions about what is normal in an unsustainable world, and the other to nail down new ideas, new principles, new language for a sustainable world, a "new normal." I hope Mark approves. And I should add that much of this was worked out through conversations and writing with two colleagues, Ray De Young and Michael Maniates, both of whom deserve more than a nod in this entire work, indeed, in all of my thinking on such matters. I hope they too approve.

Acknowledgments

This book has benefited greatly from the thoughtful read of a variety of people, some academics, some not, some young, some not so young, but all enthusiastic and helpful. All comments are greatly appreciated. Special thanks go to those who read the entire manuscript: Alan Bush, Maurie Cohen, Michael Maniates, Maria Princen, and two anonymous reviewers. For reading chapters, I thank Brian Barch, Raymond De Young, Lisa Makman, Jack Manno, Katy Manta, Paul Princen, and Detlef Sprinz. For research assistance, I thank Alan Bush and Carmencita Princen. And for special help along the way, I thank Ashley Fuller, Mike Lachance, Gabriel Thoumi, Paul Tinkerhess, and, once again, Alan Bush.

1

Within Our Means

Our global [ecological] footprint now exceeds the world's capacity to regenerate by about 30 per cent. If our demands on the planet continue at the same rate, by the mid-2030s we will need the equivalent of two planets to maintain our lifestyles. . . .

More than three quarters of the world's people live in nations that are ecological debtors—their national consumption has outstripped their country's biocapacity. Thus, most of us are propping up our current lifestyles, and our economic growth, by drawing (and increasingly overdrawing) upon the ecological capital of other parts of the world.

—*Living Planet Report 2008*

Soil degradation in one form or another now affects one-third of the world's land surface. . . . In China by 1978, erosion had forced the abandonment of 31 per cent of all arable land. . . . The United States in the twentieth century lost an amount of topsoil that took about 1,000 years to form, and currently loses 1.7 billion tons a year to erosion.

—J. R. McNeill, *Something New Under the Sun: An Environmental History of the Twentieth-Century World*

As much as 10% of global annual water consumption may come from depleting groundwater resources. . . . [By 2025], given the uneven distribution of these resources, some 3 billion women and men will live in countries—wholly or partly arid or semi-arid—that have less than 1,700 cubic meters per capita, the quantity below which people start to suffer from water stress.

—*World Water Vision: Making Water Everybody's Business*

Biologically and physically, we on this planet are living beyond our means. Economically, too, we are well beyond our means: consider current levels of personal, corporate, and public debt, as well as deferred infrastructure investments on water supply, sanitation, bridges, and roads. In terms of energy, the story is the same: over some 150 years we have grown accustomed to cheap, abundant oil, but now only the hard-to-get, energy-intensive, costly sources are left. If we turn to other fossil fuels, we are likely to bake the planet: so far we have burned the equivalent of roughly a trillion barrels of oil, enough to disrupt the climate; there is the equivalent of at least 4 or 5 trillion barrels still in the ground. Ethically, an order that bequeaths to future generations materials that present generations do not want and cannot handle—for example, nuclear waste and hormone-mimicking toxic substances—is also living beyond its means.[1]

The four *E*'s—ecology, economy, energy, and ethics—point to an order that cannot last. The next era will be one of living within our means, one way or another. The only question is what kind of order will it be.

For those of us accustomed to easy money and cheap goods and fast transport, living within our means may well seem impossible. For those coming of age in times of financial crisis and, soon enough, energy and climate crises, it may well seem unavoidable. The challenge will not just be cutting back, restraining consumption, and eschewing debt, although these will be necessary and challenging enough. Rather, the challenge will be *living well by living well within our means*.

The aim of this book is to make such living seem possible, even desirable. It is to create images of the possible—images that are realistic when the debts and deferred costs and dependencies are taken into account. It is to imagine a material system, an "economy," that is actually *economical* regarding the very resources it rests upon. It is to lay the groundwork for an *ecological order*.

So stated, this is a hugely ambitious undertaking. The requisite construction of an economical economy, one that does not waste precious resources—what I will call a "home economy"—will no doubt occupy societies worldwide for generations to come. Every step will be risky. Many people will resist, determined to make the current economy do the opposite of what is designed to do—grow endlessly.

The biggest risk, though, is not to start the new construction. It is to continue with business as usual, believing that greener and cleaner will do it. It is to pursue economic growth hoping against hope that sometime, somehow, such growth will only be abstract (in income, information, ideas, entertainment), not material. It is to extend the footprint yet further, as if we really do have a couple more planets to consume. It is to deplete freshwater as if there is a substitute for water. It is to erode soil as if this civilization, unlike all others, can do without fertile soil.

Laying Groundwork

It would be nice if the current environmental predicament were a problem of the building. That is, if we knew that the ecological, economic, energetic, and ethical problems of this grand industrial edifice, this capital-intensive, labor-saving, high-consuming, debt-laden, cost-displacing, fossil-fuel-dependent economy, were located in the floors and walls, the windows and doors, even the rafters and roof, then all we would have to do is make the repairs and get on with things. All we would have to do is divert some resources from adding rooms and verandas to fixing things. Then we could get back to normal, back to business as usual, back to growing the economy, all as if what is down below, on the ground, doesn't matter.

Unfortunately, in this particular predicament—what might be termed a "global material crisis," a crisis at once ecological and economic—all warning signs point downward. They point to the very grounding of this grand edifice. And that grounding is both human-built (the foundation, the footings and cornerstones and drainages) and nature-built (the land, the water and air and soil), neither of which can be taken for granted, nor assumed to be self-renewing. What's more, although the natural grounding can carry on by itself without the human, the human grounding cannot carry on without the natural, without resilient ecosystems and renewing flows of water and nutrients. The human system depends intimately and ultimately on the natural system. This is a biological fact that no amount of growth upstairs can invalidate.

If the above position is disagreeable, if the claims about living beyond our means, about the nature of the economy, about the priority of foundations and grounding, and about the nature of the predicament and about biological facts are anathema to you, then read no further. This is not the book for you. There are books and articles galore about green buildings, fuel-efficient cars, new fuels, mirrors in space to reflect sunlight, holes in the earth's crust to pump waste. The great bulk of the funding for climate change and virtually all other environmental problems goes to such matters, along with assessments of the state of the environment. And the great bulk of what is written on the topic (the topic being global environmental change) is about greening up the economy (this very same economy, the one that must grow endlessly) and finding technological fixes (fixes that absolve us of responsibility for finding behavioral and structural fixes, the only changes that can endure).

Instead, this book is for those who know, at least intuitively, possibly scientifically, hopefully both, that marginal tinkering will not do it; neither will further documentation of the trends, not when nearly all trends point in the same direction: down to eroding foundations. This book is also for those who have had enough documentation, enough of the gloom-and-doom. As valuable as it is to lay out the context and explain the science (see data quoted above, and more below, as examples), there comes a time when we must go beyond gloomy trends. That time is now. Citizens and policy makers alike rarely respond constructively to a barrage of scary facts and scenarios. Rather, I take it that people do better for themselves and others (and "the environment") when they roll up their sleeves and tackle a problem, however big or small their contribution may be. They do better when they are realistically hopeful, engaged, and working with others.

This book, in short, is for those who know the problem is in the grounding—human and natural—and wish to get busy laying new groundwork. It is for those who know that what is needed is not a fresh coat of paint, however green; or a new set of windows and doors, however efficient; or even a new roof, however well engineered. It is for those who, despite such realizations, find it difficult to actually see what's below, hidden as it necessarily is by all that is built on top, and who have trouble imagining what the alternative would be.

So this book is about imagining—about getting grounded ecologically and ethically. And because getting grounded is demanding, this book is also about hard work. Repairing the current edifice is, by comparison, easy, if ultimately futile. Laying groundwork is the task ahead; all signs—scientific, intuitive, experiential—point there.

Fundamental Shifts

The global climate is changing, local water tables are dropping, farmers and food distributors are not keeping up with demand, and economies everywhere, from the national to the international, are struggling. Everyone seems to agree that change, serious change, is occurring. And many are deeply worried. Others, though, say things always change. Always have, always will. We just need to adjust, improve production, green up consumption, fine-tune the economy.

To my mind, these changes are quite unlike those of the past. And what they portend for the future is quite unimaginable. My thirty-plus years of observation and study, of teaching and tinkering have led me to conclude, only in the last few years, that *fundamental shifts* are now occurring, and more are on the way.

It is not just that things are changing; indeed, they always have. It is that they are changing in ways previously unimaginable to scientists, business leaders, policy makers, and citizens alike. In the scientific community, terms like *surprise* (which now has a technical definition), *threshold* (as in, "cross that threshold and your environment is completely different"), *irreversibility* (there is no going back, no recovery), *nonsubstitutability* (things like an atmosphere and water cannot be replaced), *unprecedented rates of change* (trends of the past are poor indicators of the present, let alone the future), and that all-purpose, ever-popular *crisis* (both fast and slow): these terms are now commonplace. This is not alarmism; it is a reflection of many people's struggle to fathom fundamental shifts, changes for which there are few if any precedents, and thus unimaginable, and for which appropriate social responses are equally unprecedented and unimaginable.

So, for example, bark beetles, once restricted to two-year cycles by winter cold, are now reproducing annually. It is not just that they are devastating broad swaths of Rocky Mountain forests but that those forests may never recover. Frogs are disappearing worldwide. It is not just that it is a shame to lose species; species have always gone extinct, after all. It is that the mysteries of their disappearance, combined with their status as

amphibian "canaries in the mineshaft," due to their thin po-
rous skin, render conventional conservation irrelevant for frogs
and perhaps also for a good many other terrestrial vertebrates.
We cannot save one species at a time or even one habitat at a
time when systemic instability is the issue. Sea levels are rising, already prompting island nations and other communities
in low-lying areas to prepare to migrate. It is not that migrations have not occurred before, but that, with 6 billion people
on earth, all the good places are taken. In these cases, and in so
many more in the physical and biological realms, no one knows
what to do, except proclaim more-of-the-same, only new and
improved, greener and cleaner.

Turning to the social realm, the shifts are murkier, more con-
tested, and yet no less fundamental. A 150-year "law" of oil
supply says that when oil supplies are tight, prices go up, which
stimulates investment, exploration, and technological innovation, bringing on more supply, all of which pushes prices back
down. The cycle may take months or a few years, but it is a
cycle, as inevitable as the business cycle itself, or the life cycle.
Now, according to the International Energy Agency, the investments are not being made.[2] And even a few mainstream com-
mentators are violating a taboo: they are saying that world oil
supply has peaked, or is about to, which is to say that all the
cheap oil is gone. Whatever the case, hardly anyone predicts a
return to cheap, abundant oil.

If world oil has peaked, or when it does (after all, oil production already *has* peaked for more than thirty countries, including the United Kingdom and the United States), there is good
reason to believe the back side of the oil production slope will
not be smooth and gradual. On top of this, the price of oil (or
of the various alternatives referred to as "liquid fuels") may be
the least of our worries. Available hydrocarbons exceed what
humans have burned so far by a factor of at least four or five.

If what we have burned so far is enough to disrupt the climate, it strains credulity to believe the planet can still be habitable after burning that amount again, and again and again. All told, something has to give, and it will not be just incandescent light-bulbs and gas-guzzling cars. Again, no one knows what to do.

That economies must grow is as inviolate a truth in modern economies as an afterlife is in major religions, as elections are in democracies. Central banks such as the U.S. Federal Reserve are charged with stabilizing the currency so as to ensure growth. And not just any growth, but vigorous growth, "healthy" growth, the 4 percent or 5 percent, say, of most advanced industrial economies, and, elsewhere, even the 10 percent or 15 percent growth of rapidly developing economies such as China and India, and well above the anemic growth of a mere 1 percent or 2 percent that Japan suffered through much of the 1990s, its "lost decade." (Zero growth, of course, is entirely unthinkable.) With adroit handling of the macroeconomic levers, principally the money supply and interest rates, they have been able to influence investment, savings, production, and consumption.

Now, with financial collapse and economic contraction worldwide, it is looking like the machine, the "normal economy" that could always generate "healthy" growth, has spent itself. What's more, for "environmental issues," it is apparent that the macroeconomic levers are quite irrelevant. Macroeconomic instruments can do little to correct underlying realities—realities such as the end of cheap oil and the disruption of the climate, realities that do not, it turns out, even enter the macroeconomic calculus, that barely get expressed in prices, let alone in gross domestic product (GDP). Financial instruments can create new forms of debt, but they cannot redress the natural and social debts that pile up. And economic growth has been stubbornly resistant to decoupling from absolute levels of energy, material, and emissions growth.[3]

Now it really is about fundamentals, but not the fundamentals economists talk about—supply and demand, pricing, liquidity. Rather, today's fundamentals go to the *foundations*, to an economy's grounding in material sources—oil, water, soil, ecosystems, climate-stabilizing atmosphere—and to human capacities—a desire for economic security and meaningful work, for social engagement and neighborliness, for self-reliance and self-governance. The twentieth-century economy was normal only because it could afford its assumptions and the exploitative practices that went with them. And it could ignore consequences. It was adaptive in its time. But in our time it is fast becoming the *old normal*. It just will not do in the twenty-first century, not with 7, 8, or 9 billion people, not with the resource trends, not with current consumption rates. Proponents of the old normal have a hard time imagining that the twentieth-century economy might not be able to solve critical material problems, that markets and technologies will not rise to the occasion, that clever people with lots of resources and information and very sophisticated modeling cannot deal with disappearing ice packs, pest outbreaks, and the end of cheap oil, let alone "old problems" like poverty, disease, and hunger. For these new problems, *fundamental shifts* are in order to match the fundamentals of the *new normal*.

The New Normal

Yes, indeed, the foundations of a normal world, what we and our ancestors for generations have taken for granted, are being rocked. But the passive construction "are being rocked" is misleading. That rocking is done by agents—by us humans.

Yet not by all of us, really. The real agents are those who have written the rules and set the expectations that constitute the old normal. They are the ones who created a normal that included the following claims, however implicit—claims that are only now being tested over an ecologically relevant time period and only now being questioned for their moral grounding:

1. Endless material expansion on a finite planet is possible, indeed desirable, dependent only on human ingenuity and the willingness to print money, incur debt, and take financial risks.

2. Cheap energy will, if access is ensured, flow continuously from any and every pool, no matter the geology or culture or politics, to its highest returns, which is to say to wherever in the world buyers are willing and able to pay the price.

3. Consumer demand determines what producers make, so what is made, goods and bads, is what consumers (read, all people or society) want.

4. Risks can be managed, traded against each other and against economic production, including risks that cannot be foreseen, whose consequences cannot be contained, and whose time frame exceeds all human experience.

5. Economic, technological, and demographic growth will solve all problems, including the problems of economic, technological, and demographic growth.

These claims, built into a belief system and welded into place by theories of economic growth and technological innovation, lead people to believe, to have faith, to participate as consumers and investors, but not to question. Above all, once absorbed as normal, these claims allow no one to let on that the "old confidence" is eroding—that the game, by all physical, biological, ecological, social, and economic measures, is really a confidence game, and the con men always get out early, leaving the mess for everyone else. This is all taken as normal, because to do otherwise is to expose the con. To question the assumptions, to challenge the prerogatives, is to crack the belief system. And then it all falls down.

But when we view contemporary patterns as symptoms of fundamental shift, however uncertain their final outcome, we see that the old normal hardly needs the questioning and challenging because it is falling of its own weight. Each irreversible shift, each wobble in the legs, each failure to shore up a chinked foundation assures it. Instead, what is most needed, and what this book hopes to illuminate and lay the groundwork for, is a new normal.

The time for a new normal is, indeed, now. On the environmental front, it begins with the observation, indeed the acceptance, that contemporary trends—environmental, economic, political—lead inescapably to one profound and disturbing conclusion: the era of "protecting the environment" is over, and the era of ensuring life support has begun. For several decades now environmental action has been a good idea to some, an annoyance to others. It has been a personal virtue, a cause, a rallying cry, a self-righteous plea, a haven for do-gooders and misfits. It has been a value preference, a lifestyle choice, a contest of lobbyists and litigators. More recently, it has been a product placement, a consumer choice, a marketing brand, a bandwagon to jump on and ride to ever greater commercial glory.

No longer. "Protecting the environment"—that is, saving the odd species, setting aside the random tract, tagging the occasional pollutant for phaseout, greening an automobile fleet—is now, in light of fundamental shifts, quite beside the point. The point is (and here I reach for phrasing that itself has not been trivialized by the pervasive gloom and doom of modern environmentalism) that what humanity has always been able to take for granted—ample soil and water, a stable climate—are declining and disappearing and the risks cannot be managed in the conventional sense. The point is that present patterns of consumption are consuming life-support systems, locally and globally. The point is that what we take for normal is actually *excess*.

Yet what gets noticed as this age of excess falters is an increase in energy prices and threats to investments and jobs. Underlying it all, though, are vanishing natural resources and waste sinks (places where wastes can be deposited and eventually reassimilated), happening as if by magic. But the disappearing act is all of a piece with the energy and economic disruptions: it was by magic that we could displace costs so cleverly through the first couple of centuries of fossil-fuel-based economic expansion.

It is no longer accurate to say that the environment is "threatened." Presumably designed to convey seriousness, this military/security metaphor suggests that the battle has yet to commence, that the threateners are gathering far off in a foreign place, that if we act now we can deter or repel the attack, that life can continue if we all come together to vanquish the foe. The foe is that enemy of the environment out there (or, even more preposterously but equally logically, the enemy that is the environment itself). Of course, there is no "other" that brings ruin to our resources; we are doing it ourselves. But now, with the aid of the physical and biological sciences, we see the enemy and it is us, especially the "us" who write the rules and capture the bulk of the benefits while others absorb the costs.

Clearly we need a better metaphor. In fact, we need better language, language that situates daily decision making, individual and collective, in natural processes, language that overcomes the us-versus-them of military metaphors, the build-a-better-world of engineering metaphors, the get-the-right-price and buy-it-and-sell-it of commercial metaphors. We need language that enables living *with* nature, not living *against* nature. (See chapters 10 and 11.)[4]

Beyond the Trends, the Critique, the Lament

So what to do? For me, given the trends and the need to understand them, it is tempting as an environmental scholar to commit my work to detailing those trends, to explaining them and suggesting where they are heading. This, after all, is what most environmental science is about; in fact, it practically defines environmental science. It is also tempting as a scholar and citizen to critique those trends, to get under the skin of politicians and corporate CEOs, to probe underlying assumptions about the way the world works (and does not), to expose who benefits from the status quo and who does not. It is even more tempting, I must say, to throw my hands in the air and cry, Woe is us! (Yes, I actually do that on occasion, but only in private.) Lamenting the trends and the deep doodoo humanity is in is a favorite pastime of us environmental scholars, and of activists and policy makers. It may be a necessary personal coping mechanism, given the alarming nature of the trends. But beyond the temporary psychological benefit, it is generally not helpful.

In this book I do a bit of detailing of trends (in fact, I have done most of the "trending" already) and maybe two bits of critiquing. And I will resist the urge to cry out. Otherwise this book is not at all the typical environmental screed, or report, or analysis. It is an attempt to point forward—forward and, especially, around the corner. It is an attempt to find signposts, even bent twigs and a trail of crumbs on the path to a sustainable world.

This is an exercise, then, in "what can be" and "what should be," what in my business we call "prescription" or "policy recommendation" or "normative theorizing." I will just call it a "reasonable idea," reasonable *given* the trends, *given* the deficiencies of more-of-the-same-only-greener-and-more-efficient, *given* the human proclivities for material security (e.g., dependable, affordable, safe food, a roof over one's head) and meaningful connection via work and play and community, and *given* the ability of people to self-organize and provide for themselves. And so on.

So this is an attempt to go beyond the ubiquitous state-of-the-environment reports (which document the same trends, sometimes new ones, but almost all of which point in the same depressing direction) and beyond the listen-up-folks-this-is-serious and we've-got-to-do-something statements that often follow the reports. It is also an attempt to go beyond easy answers, beyond what often follows the "listen up" lament, to look not just a few steps forward but around the corner where extrapolations from the present tend not to go.

Looking around the Corner

There is no shortage of people who look into the future and tell us what will be and, with a few assumptions about values and capacities, what should be. But, to my mind, such prognosticators mostly gaze down the very road they are standing on. Where they stand determines what they see. Or, to put it in diagrammatic terms, prediction tends to be a simple extrapolation of a trend line, the line that has brought the predictor to the present. No other trend lines are relevant because there are no other data. Hence, the only empirically valid *prescription* is a historically established *prediction*.

Seeing the future in the past and present has a long and venerable tradition, one validated by the rigors of scientific and historical analysis. But the road we stand on today, where the ground is shifting, is not necessarily the road we will, or *should*, stand on tomorrow. The trend line of the past, with so many assumptions hidden in the data, in the historical facts, in the choices made and rules adopted, does not necessarily point to the future. It does not point to the future that will occur or to the future that we will want. In fact, that past is typically a history of facts conditioned by endless frontiers and bounteous resources. Such a past offers little guidance when there are no more frontiers—when resources are exhausted, waste sinks filled, the climate destabilized. It offers little guidance when the task is to live within our means.

Instead, we need to look around the corner. We need to search for paths to what can be. With biophysical discontinuities reported yearly (even monthly, it often seems), with economic truths shown to be falsities as cheap oil disappears forever, with public intellectuals and public officials declaring the need for "fundamental" change, the same road, however engineered to be efficient or beautified to be green, is not a promising route. Yes, we have to start from where we are. But we also have to look for the road not taken, for the route with the fewest irrelevant assumptions, the least number of diversions. Turning the corner and searching for new paths will no doubt lead to many dead ends, as all true ventures do. But our venture, I argue in these pages, is toward new ways of living, of connecting to place and to each other and to natural systems.

To turn the corner, explore new paths, and back out of dead ends requires, among other things, warning signs. In chapters 3 and 4 I put up several of these, what I call "false paths" and "central myths." In the concluding chapter, 12, I offer several more.

Toward Ecological Order

For a long time we have dealt with our biophysical environment by mining it, cleaning up the odd pollutant, and saving the occasional species (mostly the large, charismatic ones). Now humanity has a stark choice: keep on mining and cleaning and saving, all the while depleting resources and filling waste sinks and permanently compromising regenerative capacities, or live within ecological capacities.

We are climbing a mountain ridge, each step more arduous and more risky. Treading heavily, we are loosening the very path we walk on. The ridge drops off precipitously, promising great calamity should we continue the ponderous trek. There are other paths with slopes not so treacherous that offer possibilities for stability, security, and fulfillment. Those paths, at once gentler and more manageable, challenging and more fulfilling, offer a good life, albeit with a lot less power, with a lot less material and energy. But unlike the "gotta move forward" path of material progress, with its endless climbing, voracious consuming, and devious disposing, these other paths require hard choices, the willingness to sacrifice, to exercise restraint, to say no, to think long term, to self-govern and self-produce, to follow nature's principles: all very human things to do, to be sure, yet absolutely contrary to what is expected on that endlessly ascending path. What will be expected more and more as global ecological constraints tighten, is less stomping mightily, more treading softly.

So these chapters mostly locate on the gentler side, on the slopes and contour lines that still have hope, that still offer meaningful choices for individuals and communities and societies. There are no panaceas here, though—no quick fixes, no technological miracles, no green consuming that somehow displaces brown consuming. There are no lists of "simple things you can do to save the planet." Here there is hard work and long negotiations, frustrating self-organization and monotonous self-governance. Here only minerals are mined, not aquifers and soil. Here the con artists work at the circus, not on Wall Street or in the halls of government. Here people are constantly trying to figure out how to live well and live within their means: their financial means, their societal means, and, most fundamentally, their biophysical means. Here everyone fixes a gaze on the future, discounting nothing of true value, and, Janus-faced, also looks back into the past for nuggets of wisdom, dismissing no practice as necessarily "backward" or "traditional" or "primitive." Here no one dares relegate significant decisions to "the market" or to boosters of a new technology or to absentee owners or to investors who can send billions to any place in the world in seconds but who, at the end of the day, have no place of their own. Here, in short, fundamental biophysical shifts require fundamental social shifts.

In an ecological order, I will argue in the coming chapters, a society's material foundations are grounded in the biophysical; its daily practices centered on self-directed, self-restraining work, not the purchasing of goods; and its language imbued with ecological content and long time horizons. Overarching these elements is a norm against excess and an ethic for living within the society's means, biophysical and social. The material side of this order I will call a "home economy," implying, among other things, that this is an economy grounded in place.

The first step in constructing a home economy in an ecological order is to see the disorder in the current order (part I). The second step is to erect scaffolding for the home economy—organizing principles that are inherently ecological, sensitive to excess, and structured for restraint; practices that connect ecological and social values; and an ethic of the long term where thrift and prudence are paramount (part II). The third step is to acquire tools to work from that scaffolding. It is to frame problems, the requisite first step toward solving problems. Positive sacrifice, the opportunities of limits, and well-being through work are key concepts. Well-chosen metaphors and a pluralism of worldviews lead to levers for hopeful change. All of this is straightforward in many ways, yet difficult nonetheless.

The difficulty, I must stress, lies not in the complexity of the task, the vastness of the problems, or the uncertainty and risks of attempted solutions. Rather, the difficulty lies in the way problems have been framed in the old normal, in the worldviews that have, for a century or more, been fabulously successful. Successful, that is, in extracting and manufacturing and expanding. Successful in finding frontiers, in displacing full costs in time and place. Successful in producing and consuming goods, where goods are good and more goods are presumed better, all as if there are no serious bads. Successful in conflating those goods with the good life.

A new success for a new normal is now in order. For this, new framing is needed, one that leads to a worldview that fits this world, the world inherently constrained by limits of all sorts, from the biophysical to the psychological. Constructing this worldview is the strategic imperative that matches the biophysical and social imperatives. It isn't easy, but as I hope the coming chapters will show, it is really quite straightforward.

Finally, in the coming chapters the reader will not acquire a recipe or a formula, and certainly no list of "easy things you can do to save the planet." Rather, if this book succeeds, the reader will come away with a positive, realistic, grounded sense of the possible. That sense, and these concepts and tools, can be applied in the full range of citizen action, from the individual to the collective, from doing good work to running a business, from organizing a neighborhood to leading a movement, from lobbying to lawmaking. These concepts and tools are designed for imagining, and then enacting, an ecological order. They are designed to make normal an ethic of living well by living well within our means.

I

The Disordered Order

2

From House to Home: A Parable

Industrialists have built a grand edifice generally called The Economy. It is a structure so massive, so formidable, so strong and imposing that no observer, in or out of the industrial world, can help but notice. Indeed, one can't help but stand in awe of such an imposing construction. To behold such a work is to glimpse the vision of industrial grandeur: one hails the greatness and admires the ingenuity. What industrialists have built is propelled by science and technology, fueled by fossil fuels, geared by the workings of markets, and driven by consumer demand. It's a system, and it all works together. That the Great Industrial Edifice, The Economy, will endure forever, the Faithful have no doubt.

But, then, there are Doubters. When they look at the Great Industrial Edifice, they see a House of Cards. This House is indeed big and, from certain angles, quite imposing, especially at a distance. But the Doubters have an annoying habit (annoying to the Faithful, anyway) of examining structures up close. When they do, they are hard pressed to see what actually holds the Great Industrial Edifice together. Because no one, even among the industrialists or the Faithful, quite seems to know the answer to this question, the Doubters surmise that it's not mortise-and-tenon joints, not cement and rebar, not welds and rivets, not nuts and bolts. No, up close they see that it's a whole lot wispier than that. In fact, as best they can tell, what holds the Great Industrial Edifice together is . . . (and here, before saying any more, they take a deep breath), is . . . *confidence.*

Confidence takes many forms—IOUs, dollar bills, credit, debt, loans, futures contracts, derivatives. Like a children's game, building this House has been a lot of fun, especially for those who manage to put more cards on top. Among the Faithful, the industrialists certainly have worked hard, developing their skills, being clever, and exercising discipline. Some seem to have had more cards to start with. All along, leaders among the Faithful have written the rules of the game.

However they came to be on top, the Faithful always look forward, and upward, to the next course of cards. And they all share one core belief: the cards will stay up and more cards can always be stacked on top, no matter where they come from; the great game never ceases. For the Faithful, seeing is believing. And what fun!

But then along come the Doubters, bent, no doubt, on spoiling all that fun. Rather than gaze at the top, as the Faithful are wont to do, they scrutinize the bottom. They see a card table whose legs are wobbly. They see that some of the cards going to the top are actually coming from the bottom—from the foundation, as it were. They show others. They talk about what they see. Sometimes they're ignored, sometimes shouted down.

"Shhh! You'll spoil the game."

"But it's destroying itself."

"Bah! Be quiet. You'll ruin it for everyone, yourselves included. People need jobs, you know. This is The Economy. Think of the poor, the hungry. Gotta keep it going—for them."

"The poor are all at the bottom. You're up high, where the air is fresh and the view spectacular."

"They'll be here, too, soon, just as long as we keep building. The more that goes on top, the more everyone has, including those at the bottom."

The Doubters had doubts. But their concerns were not just for the poor, the unemployed. They were for the children, all children, and the children's children, and the children's children's children.

"You're consuming everything. Even the foundations."

"Shhh! Don't you understand? We have to consume to grow, and we have to grow to give people jobs and feed the hungry. This is The Economy. Don't you understand?"

No, they didn't understand. It just didn't add up, especially when all the building at the top seemed to require extracting from the bottom, like excavating one's own foundation. What kind of an economy is that?

"Not very economical," one Doubter remarked.

The more the Doubters scrutinized, the flimsier the card table appeared and the weaker the courses at the bottom became, the foundational cards as it were, the base of The Economy. The Doubters really did not understand how such a thing could persist: how a House of Cards, held together by little more than the confidence that the House will hold together (it has so far, after all!), all the while eating away at its very foundations. And they did not understand how it could even be called an "economy" when the very term refers to a *home* and the maintenance of a *household*.

So some of the Doubters stayed, pointing at the wobbles at the bottom, the cracks in the facade, and, increasingly, the teetering at the top (what the Faithful call "the flexibility of a dynamic economy"). But others wandered off, in search of another home, a real home, one they could understand, one that made sense to them, one that was secure top and bottom. That home, that economy, wouldn't "give people jobs" or "feed the hungry." It wouldn't be held together by a wish, a materialist desire with no material substance. How, the Doubters thought, still shaking their heads, could such an economy, that House of Cards, really work, for everyone, for long? They tried to put it out of mind, but its image was everywhere. They discovered a trick, though: the more they imagined the Home, the more the House of Cards faded from view.

An economy, they thought, should work because everyone works, because working—producing, creating, caring—is what holds a home together. And what would support it would not be a card table whose legs wobble with endless excavating, threatening to fold under the growing weight, but a solid grounding, a dependable substrate, along with a foundation, all grounded in place. That grounding would not be the smoke and mirrors of a confidence game but soil, ever-renewing soil, and rivers and lakes, free-flowing and self-cleaning. It would not be financial promises backed up by gold blocks or green paper or spinning electrons. It would be grasslands and forests and estuaries and coral reefs, backed up by microorganisms and macroorganisms and well-tended fires and meticulously kept compost and humus. In this economy, a "Home Economy" (a term the Doubters invented and came to like very much, despite its redundancy), people would feed themselves, because they could, because they wanted to and it was satisfying, and because they couldn't countenance others feeding them, as if they were helpless wards of the state.

A Home Economy seems so straightforward—a "real economy" based on "real estate," so to speak, the very land we walk on, the water we drink, the animals we husband (or just watch), the plants we cultivate (or just look at). Very straightforward to the Doubters, anyway. Surely a Home Economy exists somewhere. They kept wandering. And imagining.

Their explorations, mental as much as physical (or both, together), took them to many places, places that were at once new and familiar. Eventually, through no foresight or plan, they found themselves climbing a mountain. It seemed like they had been here before. Though the House of Cards was far out of sight, the Doubters felt like its spell was still with them, calling on them to climb higher, make haste, produce products and consume consumables. The path ran along a ridge, one whose sides got steeper as they went up, and thus the path became increasingly treacherous. One misstep, and down they would tumble. This, too, felt familiar; it reminded them of the precariousness of the House of Cards.

The Doubters kept climbing, as everyone back there in the industrial (waste)land was wont to do. "Gotta move forward," a voice seemed to say. "Don't look back," said another. And later, a harsh voice this time: "This isn't good enough. It's *never* good enough. Keep on trekking!"

So trek they did. At first they just continued up the ridge. It was so familiar. Every rise seemed to offer new vistas, new opportunities, new things to enjoy.

A few saw trouble ahead and issued warnings. They came to doubt that this was the only path. So they took side paths that veered off in other directions. Some of these were treacherous, and some led to a dead end. The explorers kept trying, though, doubting as always, singing and yodeling (they were in the mountains, after all) to drown out the voices.

In time, their own voices, aided by echoes from surrounding mountains, drowned out the voices of forward progress. They found a path that more or less followed a contour, dropping occasionally (sometimes unexpectedly, sometimes hazardously), and rising here and there, too. The farther they went, the more familiar the territory became.

"Haven't we been here before?" one remarked.

"It does look familiar, but I don't think so."

The path led to a valley, ringed by mountains and moraines. It was already occupied. (Everything was, because the Great Industrial Edifice ordained that every space, every nook and cranny, be occupied, that every useful thing be used to the fullest.) But here, for some reason, the occupants were few in number, and welcoming. The landscape, both natural and built, was indisputably familiar.

"I think we're going in circles."

"Yeah, aren't we back where we started?"

"Could be, but no one looks familiar. And I don't see the House of Cards."

"Maybe they dismantled it—finally."

"Or maybe it fell down."

"I get the feeling," one said after a pause, "that coming off that ridge makes us see things differently, even the House of Cards, if it's still around. Maybe what we're seeing was always there."

"Seeing the new in the familiar, perhaps?"

"Yes, something like that. Let's continue."

The band of trekkers came to a small store and decided to sit down for a cup of coffee. It wasn't a specialty coffee shop, just a small store with plain coffee and lots of other things, most, it seemed, quite useful—soap, nails, bread, milk. They took a couple of tables, worried that they might be sitting in regular customers' favorite spots. They sipped coffee quietly. And they listened.

People, some vaguely familiar, came and went, greeting each other, asking about the kids, work, the weather. They picked up mail or a newspaper or a prescription drug. And some sat down for a cup of coffee, nodding at the trekkers and whispering something, but otherwise ignoring them.

Again, the trekkers just listened.

"If the rain holds off a couple more days, I'll be haying soon."

"Me too."

"I'll put out the call."

"Won't they all be down at the lake?"

"Yeah, but they'll break for haying. The harvest always comes first."

The trekkers looked at each other. One whispered to another, "If I'm not mistaken, *this* is a Home Economy."

"Could be. We have a lot of listening to do."

And listen they did, intently, disrupted only on occasion by the now faint voices of progress and distant visions of the Great Industrial Edifice. They listened, looked, and questioned, trying to imagine a Home Economy.

3

To the Heart of the Beast

It is so easy to follow the same path, anticipating the next rise, seeking that elusive peak, listening to familiar voices. The tried-and-true path becomes a false path, though, when higher is not better, when the peak is a mirage, and when the voices mislead.

It's the Economy, the One and Only Economy

The only way we are going to get innovations . . . in energy-saving appliances, lights and building materials and in non-CO_2-emitting power plants and fuels . . . is by mobilizing free-market capitalism. The only thing as powerful as Mother Nature is Father Greed. . . .

The only way to stimulate the scale of sustained investment in research and development of non-CO_2 emitting power . . . is if the developed countries, who can afford to do so, force their people to pay the full climate, economic and geopolitical costs of using gasoline and dirty coal. . . .

The only way to stimulate more nuclear power innovation . . . would be federal loan guarantees that would lower the cost of capital for anyone willing to build a new nuclear power plant. . . .

Americans [must] understand that green is not about cutting back. It's about creating a new cornucopia of abundance for the next generation by inventing a whole new industry.[1]

—Thomas L. Friedman, columnist

Defenders of the familiar; builders who stack yet more cards on top, ignoring their origins; boosters who see great promise ahead in high-tech innovation and freewheeling markets, discounting who wins and who loses: these are people who do not like to talk about a different path. For them, there is really only one path, or a string of paths, all in a line, all straight and narrow, all beautifully engineered and perfectly managed, and all endlessly climbing. Maybe the metaphor of a multilane freeway is more apt: ever farther, ever faster, ever freer. But, we doubters must ask, farther in which direction? More production, more consumption, more material choice? And why is faster presumed better or necessary? Might a faster, endlessly consuming life *not* be a better life? And free of what? Of responsibility to others and to future generations who wish to live well on this planet? On this path, we are clearly making progress, but where are we going?

As long as the proponents of infinite growth on a finite planet keep the conversation on their terms, within their vision of endless abundance for all for all time, it continues—until the path drops off a cliff or erodes to a muddy impassable gully. And I am convinced that on this path greenhouse gas loading continues, dispersion of persistent toxic substances continues, and freshwater drawdown continues, not to mention job loss, family stress, and community decline.

So how do the defenders of the status quo keep everyone moving in lockstep up that single path? I see two major strands of that "one and only path," each with a powerful set of traffic control measures. No doubt readers will come up with more, but these two—"the economy" and "the only way"—should get us started, that is, started seeing clearly the direction of the current path. And they should get us started finding new paths: paths that rise and fall, meander, take the occasional detour and dead end, yet depend not on endless commercial growth but on working together for the good life and working together to sustain the resource base the good life depends on.

This alternate path, off the ridge and along a contour with dips and rises, is one that everyone, rich and poor, powerful and weak, can chart. It does not require experts and esoteric knowledge and huge piles of money. It does not require that we further unleash greed, force people to behave properly, or subsidize an energy source that has permanent, unwanted, and unmanageable waste. It is a path that includes growth (the rises), but growth for high purpose—for example, alleviating poverty. It includes downshifting, lowering consumption (the dips and falls) for those who are materially bloated. It includes self-directed exploration and experimentation (the meanders and detours and dead ends) to find one's own place—whether in the valley, on the hillside, or along the stream.

The two strands that compel endless climbing are so well trodden in our current political economy (I use this term to denote the entire institutional and cultural environment in which markets operate) that they seem normal, the way it has always been, the way it will always be. Such seeming normalcy comes about in part because the traffic control measures are mostly hidden—yet hidden, I hope to show, in plain sight. My aim is to turn on the search lamps and cast a bright light on these measures, exposing them for what they are: *false* paths and *false* signs to the good life, to security, to democracy, to environmental protection and ecological sustainability.

So the first strand, in this chapter, takes us right into the heart of the beast—"The Economy." The second, chapter 4, takes us into the murky water of beliefs and values and behavior change. Succeeding chapters lead us off the precipice and out of the swamp onto terra firma, from which, with ecological principles and positive sacrifice and determined work, we can build new foundations, solid ones, grounded in place for the "Home Economy," the economy of an ecological order.

Keep On Consuming!

I know we're consuming too much. We've got to cut back. But if we do, it'll hurt the economy. So how do we consume less without hurting the economy?

It is true that consumption drives the current economy. Some 70 percent of this economy, economists say, is consumption. Take that away, and the economy we have collapses. What's more, because an economy must grow, say economists, policy makers, businesspeople, labor leaders, educators, and nearly everyone else in a leadership position in an advanced industrial society, consumption too must grow. So, yes, any change in the accustomed patterns of consumption will result in serious dislocations. This is real and worrisome.

But notice a couple of things. One, this position presumes that nothing we are doing now might hurt the economy. And two, the question—how do we consume less without hurting the economy?—presumes that the economy itself is doing just fine, that when there are problems, such as a recession, what's needed is a bit of stimulus here, some productivity gains there, and it'll keep on doing what it is so good at doing—growing, providing jobs, generating a return on investments.

Here is the paradox: the economy depends on increasing consumption, but ever-increasing consumption strains ecosystems, both resources (soil and water, for instance) and waste sinks (the oceans and atmosphere). Before tackling this paradox head-on, let's turn the above question of consuming less on its head. A system that grows endlessly crashes. Think of cancer cells, debt-ridden mortgages, fisheries. It defies logic, not to mention a few well-known laws of physics (like thermodynam-

ics), to presume that with continuing growth in consumption—
that is, continuing growth in the total throughput of material
and energy through our economy—the current economy will
not crash.

So this is the first point: unendingly increasing consumption
cannot continue on a finite planet with finite ecosystem capacity, with a fixed amount of water, with slowly regenerating
soil, and so forth. No one has proven otherwise. In fact, when
the question is turned upside down—from less consumption
hurting the economy to more consumption hurting ecosystems
and the economy—the burden of proof shifts. Now defenders
of endless growth must somehow show that endless material
growth is possible, that certain laws of physics can be disre-
garded. How do they do that? Faith.

Their faith is just that—faith. Based on little more than extrapolations from the past—historically speaking, a very recent past, just a hundred years or so, a past with abundant,
cheap, and readily controlled fossil fuels, especially oil. Or it is
based on a belief that the economy will "dematerialize," which
is just a fancy way of saying that GDP will continue to increase, along with jobs and income and spending, but we will
not use more resources. It's a wonderful idea. And it's a wonder it hasn't happened. Maybe someday . . . when the prices
are right . . . and when new technologies come along to make
it all so easy. Meanwhile, back in the real world, back where
clean water and fertile soil and a stable climate can no longer
be assumed, throughput increases—hugely, beyond anything
remotely sustainable.

The defenders of endless economic growth are selling us a
bill of goods—and billing future generations for those goods.
When goods are good, the defenders say in so many clever ways,
more goods must be better. But they are not always good—not
when a billion people now are left out, barely subsisting from

day to day; not when future generations must pick up the tab for bailouts and loans and deferred costs.

Living within our means is not easy; it's hard. Postponing that day of reckoning by binging and borrowing now is easy. But it can't last. We are already seeing the effects—job loss, mortgage foreclosures, crumbling infrastructure, collapsed fisheries, global warming.

So now let's tackle the question head-on: how can we consume less and not hurt the economy? This is probably the most common question I get in discussions of overconsumption, suggesting that people accept the notion of overconsumption. They just cannot envision an alternative.

Nobody is saying that we should "stop consuming." All organisms consume. Consumption is essential to life. But there are different kinds and levels of consumption, some that sustain lives without risking life-support systems—for example, only harvesting the surplus growth in a forest—and some that degrade such systems—for example, overpumping groundwater to the point that rivers run dry.

So the real question is not "How can we continue to increase consumption and not hurt the economy?" This is like an overweight adult asking how to continue to eat more every day and be healthy. It's like an addict asking how to continue to shoot up and not lose her job. It's like a homeowner taking out yet another mortgage with even higher interest rates and expecting not to lose the house.

Rather, the real question is this: how can we consume in a way that does not undermine our economy, that does not consume the very basis of that economy, namely, its waters and soils and the atmosphere and the oceans? To ask this question is necessarily to ask how much is enough, and how much is too much. It is to ask what kinds of consumption can be sustained, and what kinds cannot. These are hard questions. Policy makers don't like them. Most citizens in a consumerist society don't either: "Don't tell me what I can and can't buy!" And to ask these hard questions is to entertain the idea that "the economy" is more than what is captured in measures like GDP and trade flows, let alone capital flows. It is to consider that the real economy is grounded in "real estate," in natural systems.

So the everyday observation that we're consuming too much and it can't continue combines with the scientific truth that no organism or species can increase its material and energy consumption without eventually crashing. All this then leads to one simple conclusion, one absolutely contrary to what one would take from the original question: the consumption of vital life-support systems cannot continue indefinitely. The consumption of *products* of that system *can* continue indefinitely, provided the system is maintained, but no advanced industrial society is currently maintaining the system. Nor are the great bulk of less industrialized societies, all trying to get on the growth bandwagon by exporting their natural wealth. Each is consuming the system. It can't go on.

Part of what is at issue here is language—not just words and phrases, but perceptions and actions. It is through language that we understand our world and enact our world, including abstractions like "the economy" and "consumption." When people speak of the economy as if it is an organism, all of us cannot help but think of the economy as being natural, a real living being. This way of thinking is typified by attitudes that now constitute the conventional wisdom: A growing economy is a strong, healthy economy. A weak economy is anemic, lethargic. It needs a stimulus. It must be revived.

In this culture, all of us tend to think that "the economy" has always been this way, or that this is *the* One Right Economy, or that it is the best economy that has ever existed. We tend to think that if we tamper with it, let alone reorganize it, we will destroy this wondrous creature, this perfect order. What's more, with current language, we feel the economy (yet not the biophysical substrate on which it all depends) is something that must be protected, preserved, kept intact, defended at all costs, even if those costs are disrupted lives, fragmented communities, and destabilized climate. It is as if this essential creature, so central to our lives, must live forever and grow forever, lest it die and we die with it.

This economy has indeed been fabulously successful—on some grounds (e.g., growing itself and enriching a few). And this economy is awfully familiar; it is hard to imagine some other economy, including a sustainable one.

But the fact is, *it cannot continue.* It is not sustainable. All the evidence, from climate change to freshwater scarcity to declining oil supplies to displaced peoples, incriminates this beast. Staying with the natural metaphor for a bit longer, no organism lives forever, let alone grows forever. No species that consumes its base can persist (think of a disease organism that completely destroys its host). It is time for a new organism, a new species, a new economic order. And it can happen and, I think, will happen, whether we like it or not, because the economy is not a living being at all; it is entirely a *human creation.* And we can create a new economy: one that fits today's needs, not the needs of past centuries, and one that fits this one and only planet.

The good news is that such a new creation, a sustainable economy, is already here, albeit only in small patches. Some patches are long-standing (the odd timber company that has always restrained its harvest to ensure harvests in perpetuity, for example). And some are emerging (community-supported farms and farmers' markets, for instance). Everywhere we look (and, yes, sometimes you have to look hard), people are consciously and conscientiously building this new sustainable economy, one farm, one store, one vehicle, one locality at a time.

So as the beast cripples itself, creative people are building a new economic system. What's needed is some appropriate language and a few good principles to help repel the beast and guide that new construction. But back to the original question, how do we cut back on consumption, or, better, what should we do about overconsumption?

First, ask the real questions: How can we consume in a way that does not undermine our economy? How can we live within our means, and live well? How can we tread softly? As hard as it may be to resist the consumerist notion that the economy depends on endlessly increasing consumption, this is exactly what concerned people must do. Consume, but only what renews, not the basis of that renewal. Eat the apple; don't cut down the orchard. Drink what flows into the reservoir; don't drain the reservoir. Burn fossil fuels and emit CO_2 (after all, we emit CO_2 with every breath), but no more CO_2 than plants absorb. And so on.

Second, consider some time-honored maxims:

• From farming: Don't eat the seed corn; don't kill the brood stock.

• From fishing: Throw back the little ones and the breeders.

• From finance: Spend the interest, not the principal; diversify your portfolio; don't put all your eggs in one basket.

• From engineering: Build to specifications, then add a safety margin.

• From economics: Produce at an optimal scale, not too big, not too small.

Third, and this may be the most important point in light of the fact that living within our means is hard: much about sustainable living is hard, but very simple. Look at the maxims above. They are intuitive, everyday, ancient, the kind of thing a thoughtful ten-year-old can grasp and explain to others: If the farmer cuts down the orchard, we can't eat his apples. If our town pumps too much river water, the river dries up. And so on.

Fourth, reject the myth of a consumer economy (and it is just that, a myth, a story made up to promote certain goals, like rapid industrialization). This myth holds that consumption feeds the economy and that it is a person's duty to keep on consuming. What beast is this economy that needs such feeding? How does consuming—using up things—feed anything? Isn't it more sensible to feed people and animals, not an "economy"? Isn't it more sensible to view "the economy" as a system of exchanges, not a living organism, as some creature that can be hurt, stimulated, revived, and fed? Isn't it more sensible to see the economy as a system that ultimately depends on other systems—natural systems and social systems? Why do people have to lose jobs and consume mindlessly "for the economy"?

The fifth and final point is this: yes, we must rethink the economy, which is hard. But I am convinced that one does not have to be an expert to do it. In fact, I know very few "experts" who will even entertain such rethinking. I suspect it is in part their training, in part that many people's personal and professional lives are wrapped up in a comfort blanket of endless growth, of wealth for all, of conflict for none. Rethinking the economy is not for the experts. Remember: rethinking the economy is hard, but much about it is very simple. And it is very doable. We create our own economies, home economies, every time we produce something (whether or not it is sold), every time we consume things (whether or not we pay money), every time we *avoid* producing or consuming things (whether or not such forbearance is for one's own benefit or for that of others or for the natural world), every time we share a favored good, care for a favored child, protect a favored strip of land.[2]

What people really need to do is escape the reasoning that leads to questions like "How do we consume without hurting the economy?" What people really need is to trust their intuition about the utter illogic of an economy that needs endlessly increasing consumption. Finally, people need to know that they create their own economies, one product, one service, one exchange, one gift at a time.

Gotta Move Forward

A second traffic control measure found along the false path of "the one and only economy" is the notion that we must continually move forward—a deceptively simple and oh so reasonable position. But, again, let's shine some light and see what meanings lurk in the shadows.

To begin, in the climate debate, after the skeptics became marginalized in the face of overwhelming evidence, the signal would go something like this:

Okay, climate change is real and it's largely caused by humans. As leaders in politics and business, we get that. And we know there are other problems like tainted food and polluted water. We get that, too.

But listen, there's no point dwelling on the past. What's done is done. We've gotta move forward.

How often does such a statement sound right (no use crying over spilled milk; the past is past), and yet somehow suspicious? What this rhetoric does is divert people's attention. It deflects real action. It lets off the hook those who have written the rules of the game—the game of endless extraction and consumption—and who themselves have profited so handsomely from that game. And it perpetuates that very same game, only with a green gloss. Here's how.

First, the very phrase *move forward* sounds reasonable. In fact, in one sense, it is the only option: one cannot go back to the past. What's more, it is very agreeable: Yes, we burned fossil fuels and warmed the planet. Yes, we consumed voraciously. But we can't go back and undo our wrongs. No point in trying. All we can do is, well, move forward.

If the phrase *move forward* has a modern ring to it, that's because it is the quintessential rhetorical expression of progress. Progressives never look back. Theirs is a steady march forward, right up that ridge, never looking back or down or sideways.

Second, the phrase is suspicious because those who use it do not spell it out. "Move forward" is a journey metaphor. We're all on a path to our destination—a distant mountain peak, say—and we've been stopped by a fallen log or we've slipped on loose gravel. Gotta pick ourselves up, dust off, and get going again—forward, of course; on the same path, of course. No mention of other paths. No questioning whether this path or this mountain is the right one.

Third, to proclaim the need to "move forward" is to claim that what we have always done is what we will always do, what we must do. And what we must do is stay the course. Progressives (and they span the political spectrum, from left to right) use the phrase to justify the status quo. It justifies the current path and absolves of responsibility those who tread this path. It lets off the hook those who have promoted endless growth and mindless consumption, who haven't a qualm about displacing the costs onto the poor and weak and onto future generations, who have manipulated and deceived others for self-gain.

And, fourth, the "move forward" order is convenient, especially in a society dedicated to progress, to seeing bounteous plenty in the future and backward misery in the past. It is a convenient rhetorical tool for painting opponents (including those of us who question the path of continuous industrial expansion and the mountain of consumer goods) as anti-progress, as ne'er-do-wells acting against all that makes modern life good.

But all kinds of "progress" are hidden in the "moving forward" rhetoric. Failures are excused, misdeeds forgiven. Everything continues, unchallenged, unchallengeable.

And for defenders of endless industrial growth, commercialization, commodification, and consumerism, it means business as usual, just greener and more efficient.

What to do?

First, whenever the term is used, assume, until proven otherwise, that it is self-serving, self-justifying, and manipulative. It cannot, needless to say, be a basis for getting on a sustainable path.

Second, do not let apologists for the status quo get away with painting the alternative to their path as going backward, turning off the lights, crawling into the cave and shivering in the dark. *There are other paths and other mountains and new valleys.* They exist. And so they are possible. One might call these alternative paths "restrained consumption," "healthy community," "sustainable living."

Externalities?

Okay, say the defenders of endless economic growth,

there's litter on the path, and some gulleys have formed. Gotta clean it up, plug the holes, plant some trees. Only one way to do this, though: invest, that is, expend resources (read, money) to clean up, to get green. Money doesn't grow on trees, you know. But it does grow all along this very path, the one and only path to material prosperity. So stay the course. Don't deviate. No one likes litter, erosion, global warming, and all that. We'll clean up, don't you worry; we just have to create more wealth.

Those problems are "externalities," the defenders say, costs external to the path and thus not attributable to activities along the path:

Consumers have chosen—freely and willfully—to tread this path. Technologies, freely chosen and developed precisely to ease people's burdens in and out of the workplace, have also arisen along this path. So it is by proceeding along this path, the tried and true path to material plenty, that we can generate the wealth to pay to clean up those externalities. This is indeed where money grows. Stay the course. Keep climbing, accumulate lots of stuff (it's called "wealth"), and print lots of money to account for it all. Only then, only with so much "wealth" (money) can we hire the workers to pick up the litter and buy the machines to repair the trail and find new technologies to ease the warming.

Listen, we too want to rid the world of these annoyances, these things that interfere with free-flowing traffic. Once we do, we can get back to normal, back to the good life, material plenty for all. We can get back to what consumers clearly want, what they've purchased with their hard-earned money: ease, and comfort, and convenience.

Such reasoning, I have found, is usually enough to shut down debate, to prevent detours. But when it does not, when greenies and foodies and other misfits (present author included) persist in staking out new territory, that is when the defenders of green get mean. They play the fear card:

Our path, our beautiful multilane freeway, naturally generates great wealth, but it's vulnerable, too. Our vehicles run along a steep cliff. Deviants who call for lowered consumption or local food or solar panels on every rooftop will send traffic right over that cliff. Or if they yell too loudly about the inequities and rising sea levels and the confidence game of modern finance, they will set off an avalanche. We all must stay the course. The economy is precarious. Messing with it is dangerous. Don't even think about it. And by all means don't talk about it.

The fear card makes it difficult to have a conversation about the core elements of this wondrous economy, this economy that is simultaneously a powerhouse and a weakling, that is rife with so many "externalities" that one wonders if they are not actually "internalities," outputs *inherent* in this political economy. Is economic growth always good? Could there be too much consumption? Are goods always good and more goods better? Might economic growth and consumption be connected to a warming planet? to disappearing forests? to diminishing fresh-water? Is the base of the economy really money, stock market readings, shareholder value, consumption, consumer confidence, investor confidence? Or could it be human and natural capital? Why is "confidence" so important in this economy? Might the "modern" economy actually be, as the trekkers believe, a house of cards, a structure built on the faith that the cards will always hold, no matter how many more we stack on top and how many we excavate from the bottom? Might the confidence that holds the cards together be the work of "confidence men," however well intentioned they may be?

These questions point up the myths and taboos in a modern, industrial economy, one supposedly driven by consumers' free choices and technology's guaranteed beneficence. They are the hard questions that must be posed if a truly sustainable economy, one committed to the proposition that societies can live within their means and that the benefits and costs can be fairly distributed, is to emerge.

What to do? Unpack two of the most pervasive traffic control measures known to humankind, two measures that, like the others, are hidden in plain sight: "Consumers rule" and "Technologies save."

Consumers Rule

About a hundred years ago, economists came up with a nifty idea—consumer sovereignty. Then and now, it served a useful purpose, an analytic purpose: assume that consumers make their own decisions, that they are autonomous, fully informed individuals who drive production through their market decisions. The result is well-functioning markets that accomplish all that Adam Smith's "invisible hand" promised: efficient allocation of resources such that no one could be made better off without hurting someone else. This assumption is useful because it aided analysis, which in turn allowed policy makers to build a dynamic, growing economy. All for the good, it would seem.

Unfortunately, the assumption slipped out of the economists' neat and tidy models and into the marketing divisions of business, government, and even education. Its original status as an analytic tool has now achieved the status of an ethic. It helps justify nearly any economic outcome, including the notion that consumption must increase lest the economy be ruined.

Here's how the reasoning goes: Producers respond to customers' needs and wants. If consumers don't want a product, they won't pay for it and producers can't sell it. What does get produced, therefore, is only what consumers want. And if there are problems—with pollution or safety, for instance—it's up to consumers to demand change. So a producer would be happy to produce wood from sustainably managed, eco-certified forests or spinach without a trace of *E. coli*, but it can't do so when the demand isn't there. And it certainly can't do so by raising prices. It's really up to the consumer. If the consumer wants different products and is willing to pay for them, then we producers are happy to provide them. The consumer decides.

What's the problem? Those who wish to expand markets continuously, those who have an abiding faith that consumption can and should expand indefinitely, get a free ride: when things go wrong, when the rich get richer, when the "externalities" are no longer trivial (e.g., greenhouse gases, persistent toxics, disappearing soil), when life-support systems around the world are disrupted (e.g., climate, freshwater), the expanders can blame "the consumer." After all, the consumer rules.

Thus, just as a sovereign king is entitled to privileges and perquisites, sovereign consumers are entitled to have their desires satisfied, to have ever more goods, and to do so all at low,

low prices. What we end up with—a large basket of goods, a basket that grows ever larger even if ecosystems can no longer carry it—is what people (translation: *consumers*, not parents, not citizens, not future generations) desire. It is a myth that has served its purpose. Now the purpose is different, and the analytic tools should be different too.

Technologies Save

As demand for transportation grows, energy efficiency will become increasingly important. Ongoing technology gains in conventional vehicles, plus a growing share of advanced vehicles such as hybrids, will produce substantial gains in the fuel economy of new vehicles.

Even so, ExxonMobil expects global demand for oil and other liquid fuels to be more than 35 *percent* higher in 2030 than it was in 2005, mostly because of transportation growth.

Meeting this demand won't be easy. We'll need to invest billions of dollars, gain access to new energy supplies, and continue to advance technology and free trade.

We'll also need to use energy as efficiently as possible. By taking these actions to ensure safe, reliable and affordable energy for transportation, we'll keep the world's economy moving forward.

—ExxonMobil, "Economies in Motion," advertisement, *New York Times*, February 28, 2008

If there was ever a single statement that crystallizes the modern approach to modern problems, environmental and otherwise, it is this: new technologies will save the day. Sung from the heights of corporate boardrooms and government mansions to the depths of labor union halls and grassroots activists' basements, this mantra holds a mesmerizing spell over the body politic, especially in an advanced industrial country like the United States. At its core is a very simple concept: efficiency. I cannot do justice to the concept in this short space, let alone offer a thorough critique of Americans' fixation on technological saviors. But bear with me as I play out some key underlying assumptions to show that the allure of efficiency is understandable, yet dangerous.[3]

Efficiency is, at root, an age-old commonsense idea. A person who extracts a resource or produces a crop with less effort does better. Applied to machines, it is a no-brainer: more horsepower, more illumination, more speed for a unit of energy expended is obviously a good thing; so is less energy expended for the same horsepower, the same illumination, the same speed. But at the turn of the last century a gentleman by the name of Frederick Winslow Taylor had an even better idea: apply the concept of efficiency not just to machines but to people, in particular to people (i.e., workers) who run machines. Soon labor became fabulously productive. And in the process, decision authority, judgment, and creativity shifted away from the craftsperson (now a mere wage earner) to managers and technologists ("efficiency experts"), those who could make technologies and workers serve their interests.

Efficiency, so successful in the workplace, soon seeped out of the factory to infuse government, land management, schooling, even worship. An "efficiency craze" took over early twentieth-century America. A simple idea, a handy means of improving production, became a goal in its own right. As such, people lost sight of why efficiencies were useful. And into that political space stepped those who would use the concept for all sundry goals: increasing wages *and* controlling unionists; replanting forests *and* clear-cutting forests; urging people to shop judiciously *and* to buy impulsively; creating a productive economy with an optimal distribution of resources *and* stimulating that very same economy to grow, and then grow some more, and more.

It turned out that for all the egalitarian and democratic promises of efficiency gains, it was those people who controlled the technologies that reaped most of the gains, material and political. What's more, efficiency, as practiced, helped lay the groundwork for a consumerist society. In the process, efficiency became a means of not just determining who gets what and how (the standard economic justification), but a means of disguising and displacing full costs. It became a way of leading everyone to believe that society is marching forward, that we are all together on that endlessly productive, ever-ascending path. In fact, though, that path is eroding, its own material ground being eaten away by false beliefs in the beneficent rule of consumers and the come-to-the-rescue promise of new technologies. In the end, efficiency is a crutch, an excuse, a diversion. It is a handy guise for those who believe that perpetual industrial expansion on a finite planet is possible, indeed, that this economy is scientific, modern, consumer-driven, and just.

Disguising and displacing the true costs of mindless consumerism and endless material growth was made possible by the technologies themselves—indeed, by the very cost-benefit ratios that efficiency gains produced. Today, corporate CEOs bent on pleasing stockholders, politicians bent on pleasing key constituencies, government officials bent on raising revenues, and environmentalists bent on raising funds can all claim technology and efficiency as the elixir for all that ails the planet. Unfortunately for the true believers, the evidence is overwhelming that nothing of the kind is happening. As efficiencies increase, so does consumption.

So what to do? Search out and scrutinize the "Consumers rule" and "Technologies save" claims. Find out who really rules, who really makes the key decisions. Find out whether the efficiency claims actually reduce environmental impacts—total, net impacts—or merely slow the rate of degradation. Then set about constructing your own signposts, ones that point away from the path of treading heavily and to the paths of treading softly.

4

Only When . . .

Let's imagine that the general populace has come to accept that the beast called The Economy (which, from other vantage points might be seen as the Great Industrial Edifice or a House of Cards) must be tamed. In fact, it must be shunted aside, put in a special, well-guarded enclosure, while a new material system, say a Home Economy, is built. Chances are, even after people fully accept the impossibility of infinite consumption on a finite planet, of trying to solve problems with the same thinking and same principles that created the problems, of eroding the foundations and calling it "wealth," of pursuing technical efficiencies when the challenges are not really technical, and so forth, chances are people will still say it won't happen. They'll say it'll happen "only when . . ."—and then a series of scenarios will spill forth.

Common to many such lists are, I believe, four claims. Things will change (1) only when there's a crisis; (2) only when leaders muster the political will; (3) only when people are properly educated; and (4) only when people's values change. These too are traffic control measures that, we will see, keep our thinking and our behavior and policies on that straight and narrow path, endlessly climbing, forever extracting, consuming, and discarding until the ground underneath crumbles away.

Let's dispose of all four claims, one at a time. From my experience, we have had enough of them.

A Crisis

People won't change until there's a crisis. They're stuck in their ways. They're comfortable. They won't do anything, even with daily reports of melting ice and starving children. That's just human nature—selfish, greedy, short-sighted.

It is true that when there is a crisis people come together. When the town floods, everyone pitches in to stack sandbags and evacuate the elderly. But to conclude that people will *only* act when there's a crisis defies logic—and a whole lot of history. I will give an example of such history, but first let's put the general point right up front:

Fundamental social change starts with (1) a few committed people, (2) new understandings, and (3) small acts that eventually confront the structures of power.

And for motive, fundamental change draws on people's basic need for meaning, engagement, and fairness.

Take slavery. For the great bulk of human history, across cultures, from India and China to Europe and the Americas and Africa, slavery was a perfectly normal practice. Indeed, it was an *institution*—a set of widely shared norms and principles, rules and procedures. And what people back then shared—rulers and commoners alike—was the idea that some people, by virtue of birth or race or nationality, would be slaves. That's just the way it was, and everyone knew it; it was beyond questioning. Always has been, always will be.

Then a dozen shopkeepers and clergy got together in a print shop in London in 1787 and said, in effect, no more; this is wrong; it must stop. So they set about gathering information on what was really happening on slave ships and on the plantations. They distributed brochures and pamphlets and lectured across England and abroad. And they introduced legislation in Parliament and lobbied parliamentarians. Maybe most significantly, they systematically undercut arguments defending the normalcy and necessity of slavery—the economic arguments (the British Empire and all who depend on it around the world will collapse), the political arguments (this is just an attempt by the opposition party to take control of the government), the moral arguments (the slaves rejoice when they leave the Dark Continent).[1]

Today we take the abolition of slavery to be perfectly reasonable, moral, inevitable. But notice that for the early abolitionists, there was *no crisis*: They were quite comfortable. Their country was riding high. Life was good. Those shopkeepers and clergy and a few noblemen simply concluded that slavery was wrong. Others might have foreseen slavery's demise due to economic trends or movements for democracy and individual rights. But for much of this early history of abolition, *there was no crisis*.

Instead, a few people acquired new understandings, took a strong moral stance, and confronted power. They took on one of the most pervasive, most accepted, most "necessary" structures in human history—slavery. And they did not back down when defenders ridiculed them, when some claimed that the economy would collapse and people would be thrown out of work, that the empire required it. The abolitionists spoke truth to power. And the truth was that Britain and the world as a whole would do quite well without slavery. In fact, if one accepts the maxim that slavery degrades slave and slaveholder alike, Britain and the world did *better* without slavery. But notice: there was nothing normal or inevitable, and certainly nothing moral, about slavery.

Today there is nothing normal or inevitable about unending growth on a finite planet. There is nothing normal or inevitable about 10 percent of the world's population holding 85 percent of global household wealth[2] while a billion or two struggle day to day just to survive. There is nothing normal or inevitable about knowingly degrading ecosystems, permanently extinguishing entire species, causing irreversible changes in climate, or dislocating millions of people by failing to stop the resultant rise in sea levels. And there is nothing normal or inevitable about justifying all this in the name of "economic growth" or "progress" or "consumer demand" or "efficiency" or "jobs" or "return on investment" or "global competitiveness."

So yes, many people in advanced industrial countries are comfortable. They appear unlikely to change until a crisis affects them personally. They have done well by the current structures, economic and political. But just a bit of reflection, a glimmer of foresight, a glance at the biophysical trends, not to mention at financial trends where mounting debt threatens the entire confidence game, and the path's end point is clear: collapse.

All the market forces and technological wizardry will not change some basic facts: we have one planet, one set of ecosystems, and one hydrologic cycle; and each of us has just one brain, one body, and one lifetime. Limits are real.

If the current system cannot continue on one planet, just as slavery could not continue with trends in democracy and free markets and religious rights and human rights, then the action is with those with a bit of foresight, those with a vision of a different way of living on the planet, of living *with* nature, not *against* nature. The action is with those who can accept limits— indeed, *embrace* them.

So readers of this book, I assume, may be comfortable, but they are not content. They are looking ahead, they are concerned, they are looking for change. And they know that a fundamental shift is inevitable. They know that all systems, from organisms to ecosystems, from household economies to global economies, have limits. They are the ones preparing the way, laying the groundwork, devising the principles and, yes, the technologies and markets that will allow everyone to live within immutable ecological constraints. They are the ones making sure the sand and the sandbags are on hand so that others can pitch in when the time comes. They are the ones building the compost piles, collecting the information, experimenting with new forms of community, speaking truth to power.

The others, the people who need a crisis to act, are not the leaders. They will eventually act, to be sure; they will act when personally threatened. But they will need guidance. They will need role models, concrete examples, opportunities to engage and do good as they protect themselves. And they will need enabling language. That's where the real leaders come in. And now is the time to prepare—not when the crisis hits home and hits hard.

So make no mistake, some people will act when there's a crisis. But many others will be getting ready now. These are the concerned and committed, the "moral entrepreneurs" who are already discovering that acting now is very satisfying, very engaging. It's hard, yet at times quite simple.

Political Will

Just as it is certain that within most of our lifetimes we'll be consuming less than we do now, it is also certain that per capita consumption rates in many developing countries will be nearly equal to ours. These are desirable trends, not horrible prospects. In fact, we already know how to encourage the trends; the main thing lacking has been political will.[3]
—Jared Diamond, geographer

We are probably going to cope with a temperature increase in the range of 3 to 4°C, which means that adaptation policies should be considered together with mitigation policies. On the bright side there are some no regret policies which can be implemented immediately and which are badly needed. Energy efficiency is an obvious one. Nuclear may be another one, at least in some countries. All what is needed is strong and sustained political will.[4]

—Claude Mandil, former executive director of the International Energy Agency

The "lack of political will" lament may be the mother of all diversions. When a scholar and a leader of a powerful international agency say that we know what to do and all we lack is political will, our ears should prick up. This is political rhetoric at its best, that is, at its best diverting attention from what's really going on. There are subtleties to this "lack of political will" lament, so bear with me as I work through its special features.

International development specialist Robert Chambers once said that "lack of political will just means that the rich and powerful have failed to act against their interests."[4] In other words, if there is a "lack of political will" when, for example, the nations of the world fail to act decisively to reduce greenhouse gases, it really means that those who are actually making the decisions are acting according to their own interests, that is, according to their own narrow self-interest. World leaders, governmental and corporate, do very well by the status quo. They actually have abundant political will; it is just the will to keep the current system going. And they have the wealth and power to make it happen. They write the rules of the game. They mine one fossil fuel after another. They do not question the prerogatives of wealth and power, including their own wealth and power. They simply concentrate and perpetuate that power and that path of endless economic growth and impulsive consumption and needless depletion and gargantuan waste and horrendous imbalance of wealth between the haves and have-nots.

Chambers goes on to say that this "lack of political will" lament "is a way of averting eyes from the ugly facts"—ugly facts like who actually benefits from current patterns of over-consumption, and who actually loses, now and into the far future. Ugly facts like extreme wealth among thousands, abject poverty among billions. Ugly facts like extreme floods and fires, like disappearing rivers and groundwater, like grain and medicine shortages.

"Lack of political will" puts the burden of finding a new path on the very people who have benefited so handsomely from the current path. As long as those of us who are committed to finding a new path fall for it, we will be frustrated. We will cheer each new market development—another generation of fuel-efficient automobile engines, a new "sustainable" fuel, an "eco-friendly" cleanser—and then wonder why the path looks the same, why the trends persist, why it seems like we're about to head over the cliff.

"It is a convenient black box," Chambers concludes. Convenient for those who wish to deflect attention. Convenient for those who divide the world between good guys and bad guys. Convenient for those who see in the failure to act only igno-rance and stupidity (if only those leaders knew what I know, they'd do what I'd do), not the exercise of power. As I see it, the last few generations have seen enough convenience; it's time for hard work, even sacrifice. Calling out the lack-of-political-will lament is another hard step onto that other path, a step to reversing the trends, living within our means. At the same time, I fully expect, it is a potentially rewarding step. Even more re-warding, we will see shortly, is positive sacrifice and good work (chapters 7, 8, and 9).

People Must Be Educated, Their Values Changed

According to this false path, the problem is people and their individual acts, their selfishness, their ignorance, their narrow-mindedness, their "wrong values." Once we change those values, everything else will fall into place . . .

Along this path we find two common traffic control measures. The first is education:

Education is the answer. We have to reach young people. Tell them what's happening. Get them to see that we're in trouble, big trouble. Society needs a total transformation in values. And that has to start with the young—in high school, grade school, even preschool!

Let me say right from the outset that I am sympathetic to this argument. I am, after all, an educator. But as an educator I am also sensitive to the uses and abuses of formal education as a solution to society's ills. So as I address this path and try to expose its treachery, bear this in mind: I am sympathetic at the same time that I am critical. And I am desperately trying to be constructive, to show what exactly the role of formal education is, or should be, in the face of global ecological crisis.[6]

The "education is the answer" mantra has a certain plausibility: if society's dominant understandings and values are those of consumption and more consumption, of tearing up woodlands for housing tracts and filling marshlands for strip malls, of growing the economy to solve the problems of a growing economy, then yes, understandings and values must change. And if people acquire these values when they are young, then we do indeed have to reach them when they are young.

But let's examine this reasoning more closely. First, like all good social analysts, we must ask the "who" question: who are the "we" who would reach the young? More often than not, the "who" are those people who are aware and concerned. But who else? Teachers? Aren't they already aware and concerned and in positions of influence? No, not many of them, at least not on the issues that drive this book. So the teachers need to be educated first, which means the first step is not youth at all, but adults. Already the reasoning of this "Educate the young" measure has broken down.

But let's go a step further. As far as I know, the greatest influences on youth's values come from, first, parents, then peers (especially in the teen years), then the media. Once again, the target of education becomes elusive.

There is, though, a glimmer of hope. Let's consider peer groups. For whatever reason, there is a small segment of youth who are aware of and concerned about global trends in environmental degradation. My experience and that of many colleagues, along with survey studies, reveal that this segment is growing, and growing rapidly. As the contradictions of the present order mount (e.g., let's borrow from the future to finance the bailout today of those who played loosely with other people's money; let's blast off more Appalachian mountaintops so we can burn coal and hope that, someday, someone will figure out how to securely put carbon dioxide, a gas, underground, maybe where the coal, a solid, or oil, a liquid, was; let's grow the economy to solve problems of the growth economy, and so on), more youth will follow the lead of this segment. (In fact, this book is, in no small measure, written precisely for this segment.)

So this segment of youth does not need "new values." These young people can see as well as anyone (and certainly better than those with fossil-fuel lenses) that the current order is broken. What they need is a new vision and new language and answers to the tired old assertions of the past, of the fossil-fuel past, of the technology-and-efficiency-will-solve-all past, of the endless frontier and noble imperial past.

Finally, the "education is the answer; we must reach the youth" prescription is a dodge. It is a convenient means of shirking responsibility for one's own contribution to societal and planetary overconsumption. It is a way to continue avoiding a confrontation with the sources of the problem. In effect, it says:

I, a member of the "older generation," have tried to do my bit to protect the environment. I've recycled and sent checks to nature organizations. I hike in the woods. And I'm comfortable. But something fundamental is wrong. I don't really understand it. And I certainly don't know what to do. So let's hand this hot potato to young people. Maybe they can figure out how to undo the mess. We'll teach them all about the mess.

That is a cop-out (as this author, a card-carrying member of an "older generation," would say). That is a failure of imagination. All of us, young and old, can do better than that—maybe especially those who are more comfortable and, in many ways, have less to lose.

In some sense, my entire aim in this book is to spark that imagination, for both young and old. It is to create images of the possible, images that are generally free of gloom-and-doom scenarios (chapter 12). And my aim is to urge a confrontation with the destructive structures of material power—once again, for young and old, and without the dodge, without the excuses, without the tired old clichés that imply that experts and people in power will somehow solve everything for us.

Here in part I, then, we have looked at the disorder in the current order. Key ideas have included the rhetoric of the one and only economy and misleading claims about social change. Now it is time to imagine an alternative—the primary aim of this book. That alternative is what I have introduced as the "home economy." Central to this economy are organizing *principles* that are inherently ecological, sensitive to excess, and structured for restraint; *practices* that connect ecological and social values; and an *ethic* of the long term where thrift and prudence are paramount.

II

A Home Economy

5

Principles

Fishermen are an intensely competitive lot. One person's catch is the other's loss. Knowledge of deep pools, rocky ledges, and migration routes is acquired only through long hours on the water and is jealously guarded. And on intensively used fishing grounds, where locations are always difficult to pinpoint and boundaries are notoriously uncertain, gear gets tangled.

Lobster catchers on Monhegan Island, fifteen miles off Maine's midcoast, are no different. But unlike most high-seas fishermen, Monheganers all know each other, and they all live within a few miles of each other. And they depend on each other, on and off the water. What they have—indeed, what they have cultivated over the decades—is a community. That is not to say they all like each other; they do not. And it is not to say they work together; they mostly do not. Every boat captain is an independent owner-operator, beholden to no one but the spouse back home and the mortgage company on the mainland.

For all this, though, they do recognize a certain interdependency that others do not have, or tend not to see or acknowledge or value. Two stories illustrate how competition and community go hand in hand and, in this case, how the two help secure livelihood and ecological integrity. They also illustrate how principles of self-organization emerge in an arguably sustainable system.

It was early in the fishing season that John Murdock had all his traps in the water, each carefully placed to lure lobsters out of their hiding places or to intercept them in their offshore migrations. Many of his traps were near rocky outcroppings, close to shore. Like the other lobster catchers, every day he would go out and check a number of his several hundred traps, haul them up one by one, rest each on the starboard rail, open the wire cage, pull out lobsters one at a time to check for size and sex, rubber-band the claws of the keepers (so they would not eat each other), and throw them in a box.

One day his son came down ill. At first he and his wife, Winnie, thought it was a common childhood illness, but it got worse. They had to make a trip to the hospital, on the mainland—a long ferry ride and a drive inland. They left quickly, hoping to get back in time to do the daily chore of tending the traps.

On the way, John and Winnie heard reports of a storm brewing. Gale-force winds and big waves, not uncommon, could wreak havoc on traps, especially those set near rocky shores in shallow water. There was no turning back now, though. So as soon as John got onshore, he called a fellow lobster catcher and asked if someone might be able to move his near-shore traps.

"They're all moved," the other fisherman said.

John was at a loss for words.

"All your traps are in deep water, safe. Don't worry."

John and Winnie returned to the island a few days later, their son well. John immediately hopped in his boat and steamed out to check his traps. Sure enough, they were all in deep water; none were lost. And as he pulled them up one by one, he discovered that they were all full of lobsters, each one with its claws banded.

One might see what John's fellow fishermen did as what we would all do. When the flood strikes, we all stack sandbags;

when someone is injured, we all take turns providing meals. But consider that each of these fishermen is John's competitor; what he catches, the others do not. Furthermore, when a storm comes up quick, everyone scrambles to save gear and stay safe. One can only imagine how they coordinated among themselves to protect and tend John's traps. Still, one might dismiss the episode as an isolated incident. But another incident, an annual ritual with serious economic repercussions, suggests that it is not. It suggests that these fishermen actually have figured out how competition and community go hand in hand. And as we will see, they have figured out how to restrain their harvest to ensure a harvest, year after year, decade after decade. This is a community economy that fits the community of lobsters. Its principles—protect the community, for instance, and restrain the harvest—constitute what one might call sustainable practice in an ecological order.

The annual ritual is Trap Day, a seemingly minor piece of Monhegan's fishing practices. The season officially begins January 1, but if gale-force winds are blowing or one fisher is ill or a boat's mooring has been damaged, all lobster catchers wait. Such restraint may appear minor—only a day or two out of a six-month season—but its effects are important, especially socially. To collectively agree not to fish is to make a commitment to each other. Commitments are just words unless they incur real costs. Not to fish is a form of commitment because every day missed is forgone income. Everyone still must finish the season by sundown, June 25. Deciding collectively when to start is to annually visit the possibility of self-imposed limitation, of restraint above and beyond that which is legally mandated. To delay the season's opening conveys a sense of being in the business together when otherwise each fisher is an independent operator striving for a large and secure income. Having a flexible, self-designated start date still allows for individual initiative and competition with each other once on the water. But it helps create a level playing field; it prevents anyone with a bigger boat or greater risk-seeking propensity from gaining an unfair advantage by being the first to go out. A flexible start date thus reduces inequities of access to capital and technology, what is otherwise so common in fisheries everywhere. Conversely, a start date that is *only* legally mandated, one that is not collectively decided by the resource users themselves, is not just *a*social but *anti*social. It forces everyone to go out at the same time, regardless of weather or readiness. In that case, restraint makes no sense individually. There is never enough, just the most possible. On Monhegan, though, restraint is a given, just as the limits of the resource and the community's ability to live off that resource for the long term are givens.

Whether it's the occasional storm or the annual Trap Day, these lobster catchers have figured out how to coordinate among themselves, not because the law says they must, nor because an authority or an owner orders them, but because it makes good, rational sense. Underlying that coordination are *principles*, some commonplace in a modern industrial society—efficiency, for instance—and some quite odd, at least odd from the perspective of an economic order obsessed with growth and speed and "the next big thing."

I wish to make three points in this chapter. First, humans, as social creatures, organize themselves around principles, and those principles matter a lot for maintaining the status quo and for making fundamental shifts. Second, the principles of the current order are not up to the task of living sustainably on this one planet; new principles, and hence new organizing, is in order. Third, principles for a "home economy" in an ecological order must be inherently ecological: against excess and for restraint.

Fun and Games

Imagine you are given charge of a group of children, say, ten-, eleven-, and twelve-year-olds. You take them to a park they have never been to and tell them they have the afternoon to do anything they want (as long as it's safe). What's the first thing they do? They wander. They explore. They check out every tree and rock. Eventually, though, someone will yell out, "Let's play hide and seek!" (or tag or kickball or capture the flag or whatever is popular at the time). A few agree and someone calls, "That rock will be home, the tree's first base." Another calls, "No, the rock should be first base and the tree home." An argument ensues.

Studies show that children spend up to 50 percent of their play time arguing. Adults find it exasperating: "Will you stop arguing and just play!" What the adults do not understand but child psychologists (and probably quite a few kids) do understand is that arguing *is* playing, or at least a big and important part of it. What's more, arguments over home base and first base, over who goes first, over what's in bounds and what's out, inevitably shift: You can't do that! Why not? It's not fair. Yes it is. Well, that's not how we did it before. So? And so forth. In other words, the arguing shifts from rules to principles, to questions of what is fair, who should benefit, what is the precedent. Kids can't help but invoke or create principles. And as it turns out, adults can't either. We are, after all, social creatures.

Now consider a different game, with different players, and different rules and principles. It is a game that, for all I can tell, is a lot of fun. It's called international trade. For centuries the rules were pretty clear: I strengthen my nation by putting up barriers to imports so as to protect my industries and then strike separate deals with one country after another to accept my exports. This mercantilist order worked for a long time, at least for those who played the game best (and enforced the rules). But when too many players insisted on coming out on top, the Great Depression and a world war ensued. In the last years of World War II, policy makers, economists, and diplomats gathered in Bretton Woods, New Hampshire, to say, in effect, never again. Never again would the world descend into such anarchy because of mercantilist trade practices. A new trade order had to be created.

I will skip the details and jump right to the punch line. The trade experts may have begun with a list of rules, but they soon discovered that it was principles that mattered: rules can come and go, just like laws and regulations domestically, but principles, like constitutional provisions, are the bedrock on which all practices rest. So the negotiators came up with three core principles for the new trade order. Notice how each follows from the experiences of the past. Notice, moreover, how the principles fit the needs of the times: discouraging protectionism and promoting economic growth, all to avoid a worldwide economic collapse.

The first principle was liberalization: all nations would strive to bring down trade barriers, not erect them. The second was nondiscrimination: if a country traded a good with one country, it would trade with all others; no special deals. And the third was multilateralism: exceptions to liberalization and nondiscrimination would require agreement by the entire international community of trading nations; no unilateral moves.

One can agree or disagree with the outcome, the free trade regime of the past half century, with its multilateral agreement (GATT, or General Agreement on Tariffs and Trade) and its coordinating body (the World Trade Organization). But the point here is that what does not work in one era—mercantilism in the early twentieth century—can change to something else in a new era—free trade in the late twentieth century; it's all a matter of principles (and a lot of hard negotiating, implementing, monitoring, adjudicating, and enforcing). And it's all a matter of choice: at present, we as a society can choose to continue along the same path, the one ever ascending, ever more treacherous, ever dependent on endlessly increasing consumption and cost displacement. Or we can choose to veer off onto a gentler slope with fewer cliffs and more fertile valleys and create a different order.

So principles matter—hugely. From the playground to the trade floors, principles set the stage; they guide behavior, they enact values. They are the grand "should" statements. They are successful, moreover, if they fit the needs of the times. Back then, the issue was prohibiting competitive trade practices and preventing economic collapse all via international cooperation and economic growth. Now the issue is saving the planet's life-support system.

So now the question before humanity is what principles can guide us away from ecological calamity and onto a sustainable path. Before offering my list, let's first consider how current principles are not up to the task, how the fun of the past is the scourge of the future. Exposing the old principles is a first step toward rejecting them and adopting better ones, ones that fit the needs of these times.

Old Principles

The political economy (I use this term, recall, to denote the entire institutional and cultural environment in which markets operate) of today is supremely well organized, and thus embodies organizing principles, to do the following:

1. Extract raw materials rapidly and thoroughly (the efficiency principle);

2. Convert those materials into products that people will buy (the consumers-rule principle, chapter 3);

3. Create markets everywhere (the growth principle);

4. Dispose of the wastes in the least costly, least visible manner possible (again, the efficiency principle, along with the out-of-sight-out-of-mind principle);

5. Do more and more of all this and do it faster and faster, cheaper and cheaper (the growth, efficiency, and cheaper-is-better principles).

These are the very principles that got us into the current predicament. It defies all logic to think that the same principles will get us out—that they will do the very opposite of what they were chosen for. Instead, these principles lead would-be environmental saviors to say, in effect, "Let's grow our economy with green products and pollute more efficiently; after all, consumers are buying it all." They are buying, in truth, a bill of goods, an economic system that says, Trust us; have confidence that more consumption will be better consumption, that more efficiencies, despite their track record, will reduce the strain on ecosystems; that it's okay if a few get fabulously wealthy, because you will too, someday, somewhere, somehow. They are buying a political economy that knows no bounds, that celebrates excess, that acts as if we have a few more planets to burn. They are buying a juggernaut that rolls over the landscape screaming "growth" and "progress" and "jobs" as it leaves destroyed communities—ecological and social communities—in its wake.

The creation of a sustainable economy requires that the juggernaut be stopped before it is too late, and overhauled, if not junked altogether. Then we need to build a new vehicle. For that we need new principles, just as trading nations needed new principles after the grand failure of the old mercantilist trading order. And just as old principles wouldn't do then, the principles of efficiency, growth, consumers-rule, out-of-sight-out-of-mind, and bigger-faster-cheaper won't do now. We need principles that fit the needs of the times—namely, living on the regenerative capacities of current resources and waste sinks. In short, we need principles that are "ecologically consonant," attuned to how ecosystems actually function.[1]

Principles for a Home Economy

Here are four principles for a home economy in an ecological order. They are not as neat as those on most playgrounds or at WTO headquarters, though. I wish they were. I also wish the old principles would just die a natural death, leaving for us survivors only the task of creating anew, not deconstructing, rejecting, resisting, countering, fighting, *and* creating anew. But the proffered principles do deal with excess, a defining characteristic of the current political economy, and they do derive from established, arguably sustainable practice. So consider these provisional—not quite the Bretton Woods of sustainability, but then also not the same old same old, greened up, efficiently packaged, and sold in bulk with a big price discount.

1. The Intermittency Principle

My family has been hanging laundry on the line for quite a few years now. Our neighbors look askance, but we do it anyway. (I think it's the environmentally correct thing to do; my wife thinks I'm too cheap to buy a drier; our kids thought for a long time that it's normal, until they talked to their friends.) Thundershowers are common here in Michigan, so we cannot always have sun-dried clothes when we want them. In fact, a ritual conversation around the house goes something like this: What's the forecast for tomorrow? Better get the whites out now. But I need my blouse tonight! Too late. Ok, I'll wear the beige one—again! And so on. In other words, we wash and dry according to the weather. Sometimes we go without. Sometimes we celebrate several sunny days and our ability to clear out a backlog of dirty clothes. Most people we know do laundry when they need to; the machines and the electricity are always there, so dependable, so constant in their ready service. Our practice looks like sacrifice, the negative, do-gooder kind of sacrifice. But their laundry doesn't smell nearly as good. And our electric bill is, I'm guessing, a whole lot lower (okay, I am cheap).

When all is said and done, hanging laundry to dry, anticipating future use, forgoing immediate service is not such a big deal. It really does feel normal. Elsewhere, though, in the "real economy," unlike in our meager "household economy," normal is quite another thing.

Energy experts lament the fact that solar and wind energy are intermittent. From CEOs and engineers to policy makers and environmental activists, they all seem to agree that this intermittency is a terrible deficiency. But it is so only if one assumes that energy in our homes and stores and factories should be continuously available, uninterrupted and perfectly controllable, which is to say, like a machine. It is to assume that we, as its users, its end consumers, should never have to wait, never be without, never plan ahead, which is to say, we should be like a cross between a robot and a toddler. What energy experts see is, at best, a juvenile world, one where every impulse must be answered, every craving addressed, every desire satisfied. An economy so structured is an immature economy, one that takes as normal only what machines (if they could think) and immature humans would see as normal. It is a use-it-up-and-buy-some-more economy that is not economical at all (chapter 7). It is a wasteful economy, hugely wasteful, and not just of resources but of people's ability to participate, to connect, to find meaningful work (chapters 6, 8, and 9).

A mature economy would indeed be economical, ecologically, socially, and psychologically. It would demand of its participants, its producers and consumers, as much as they demand of it. It would be demanding in a way wholly unlike the way it is today: consumers demand comfort, convenience, speed, and low prices, and producers comply, no questions asked.

Intermittency is one such demand from nature. When the sun shines, we hang laundry and solar cells generate electricity. When the wind blows, the laundry dries faster and the windmills pump more. When it's dark we go to bed, and when it's light we get up. When it's summer, we have fresh strawberries and green beans. When it's winter, we have strawberry jam and canned beans. An intermittency principle thus says that ecological services need not be continuous, let alone ever-abundant and cheap. Instead, they should fluctuate with natural and social rhythms.

An intermittency principle would also allow for demands from those in need. When brownouts roll through a region, ball games and arcades would stop, while hospitals and fire stations get full power. When rice is scarce, the wealthy, those with other staples to eat, would do without rice. When floods decimate downstream communities, upstream communities would offer time off to help out.

Demands from nature and demands from those who need help: this is *true demand*, at once reciprocal and economical, the mark of a mature economy and a mature polity. And I dare say it makes good old common sense. Moreover, this demand says there is no pride in being treated like a machine, no good reason to live like spoiled brats. It says we can "sacrifice" (i.e., make positive sacrifice) as a matter of daily practice and public policy (chapter 8). It says we can enact an economy of care, of doing well by doing less than the most possible. This takes us to the next principle: sufficiency.

2. The Sufficiency Principle

Returning to Monhegan Island, imagine this scene: a lobsterman is standing at the starboard side of his boat, a wire trap on the rail, and he's throwing a lobster back in the water. Imagine further that the lobster is perfectly healthy, the kind many people would love to have on their dinner plate with melted butter and a bread roll. This lobsterman set that trap with warp line and a colored buoy a few days earlier, after hauling it from his island home to his boat and then out to sea. He probably hauled the trap up several times, each time checking for lobsters and making sure there was enough bait, a hunk of nicely rotting fish carcass. And he did all this, most likely, in the dead of winter with a biting wind.

Now why on earth would he throw back the very thing he worked so hard for and took such life-threatening risks to procure? One reason is that the lobster might have been too small, according to state regulations. But then, in the past that never stopped anyone. Fishermen would just take the small ones home for dinner or chop them up for chicken feed. Another reason is that the lobster might have been too big. But in the past that just meant they would sell it to a local restaurant and fetch a premium price. Or the lobster might have been an egg-bearing female. But in the past fishers would just scrape off the eggs. (Now they notch the tail fin and throw it back to signal future lobster catchers that it is female and fertile.)

In short, what was *normal* in the past—"Take every lobster caught and use it profitably somehow"—has shifted to "Take only what doesn't hurt the brood stock and hence future lobster catching, and do so for yourself and for everyone else out there on the water working their tails off, risking their lives." How this shift occurred is a long story,[2] but it does represent a very important fact, not only about fishing but also about humans' ability to adopt new organizing principles, and not just any principles but those that exemplify restraint, that orient human practice to fit ecological capacity.

On this particular island, Monhegan, that restraint has taken several forms. Not only do lobster catchers throw back lobsters that are too small or too big or fertile; they also impose a six-month season on themselves. And when everyone up and down the coast was increasing the number of traps they set—as many as two thousand traps for a boat—causing a mutually destructive arms race of traps, Monheganers decided to limit their traps to six hundred per boat. On top of all this, the state stipulated that only traps could be used, not trawls or submersibles or nets. The curious thing is that this lobster fishery is the healthiest in the North Atlantic, healthy biologically and healthy economically. This is curious, at least, to those who believe the best fishing is the most efficient fishing, the fishing that makes the most use of the resource and expends the least effort possible and generates the greatest return on investment (monetary return on monetary investment, that is).

All of this is sufficiency in practice. It is *doing well by doing a little less than the most possible*. It may not be as profitable as it could be. It may not bring the maximum conceivable catch. But these sufficiency practices are not second best, either. They are first best, *given* the desire to maintain the fishery, the lobster communities and the human communities that depend on them, and given the desire to do so into the indefinite future.

So what is the sufficiency principle? Intuitively, it is that sense of enoughness and too-muchness. It is a sense self-evident at two extremes of scale. At the individual level all of us know when we've gotten enough sleep or eaten too much; at the planetary level, from the astronaut's view, we see that the earth's thin skin of life, like our own skin, can be perturbed a bit, but certainly not too much.

Organizationally, sufficiency goes beyond the intuitive to pose questions of enoughness and too-muchness in day-to-day operations. Sufficient organizations and, for that matter, a sufficient economy routinely challenge the tendency to grow beyond one's means at the same time they look for opportunities to take downtime (e.g., the six-month off season on Monhegan) and build in a buffer against overuse of a resource (e.g., the six-hundred-trap limit).

Sufficiency thus aims at excess. It is not sacrifice in the negative sense of the term (chapter 8), not second best. It is first best when users want to do well now and into the indefinite future. It lies at the heart of an ecological order.

3. The Capping Principle

Cap-and-trade programs for emissions reductions are well known and broadly accepted. Implementation, especially of carbon emissions, is still contentious, but the idea of setting an upper bound on pollution (the capping being the ecologically significant piece of cap-and-trade, not the trading) is widely acknowledged. Target loadings is a similar concept: biological pollutants (e.g., sewage, phosphorous, nitrogen compounds) can be introduced to an ecosystem only to the point of assimilative capacity. If the target is set according to downstream assimilative capacity (e.g., in the case of acid rain, the buffering capacity of downwind alkaline soils and bodies of water) and the cap is not set to status quo emissions (often the "politically acceptable" target level), then the cap is ecologically grounded and thus a first-order principle for an ecological order.

Emissions, though, are only one realm where biophysical capacity limits must be matched by caps on human activity to ensure long-term resource use. Harvest rates tend upward for economic reasons—short-term returns on investment increase, for example, as forest rotations shorten and fish nets lengthen.

A cap on harvest rate indicates that regenerative capacities of populations and, most important, of entire ecosystems—forests and fisheries, for example—are limited, unlike the seemingly unlimited capacity of industrial systems such as monoculture tree plantations and fish pens. Water use is an obvious area for caps: to ensure long-term water security, the withdrawal rate cannot exceed the recharge rate.

If caps on emissions, harvest levels and withdrawal rates make sense—ecological sense, that is—then under certain conditions, so would caps on entrants, consumption, technologies, and even GDP and trade. That is, caps make sense on all that tends to increase throughput, all that disguises full costs in time and space and diverts attention from fundamental shifts. The primary condition would be a tight, demonstrable link to limited ecological capacity. What is more, the limiting case for caps is, at one end of the organizational spectrum, a ban or prohibition. Processes that are fundamentally unecological, that generate non-assimilative waste (e.g., nuclear waste), that cause irreversibilities (e.g., habitat destruction that drives species extinct) have no place in an ecological order. At the other end of the spectrum, there are activities and substances that, having no inherent ecological content, require no capping. Freedom, artistic expression, democratic participation, human rights, parental love, and sport are examples. Every activity in between requires some kind of limitation, some kind of check to function within the ecological capacities on which that activity depends.

In general, then, when human activities are inherently constrained by biophysical conditions, when limits exist, capping those activities according to ecological functioning enables sustainable practice. Conversely, not to impose caps, even on distal processes such as technology or consumption, is to invite depletion and irreversible diminution of ecosystem services.

4. The Source Principle

The source principle says that it is prudent to preserve the source. People can mine and manufacture, commodify and discard, but a sustainable society cannot destroy the source—a river's headwaters, a grassland's soil, a reef's coral, a forest's seed trees, a fishery's spawning ground, a grain's genetic stock, an atmosphere's chemical integrity.

The source principle actually plays out routinely in the economic realm, the dominant realm of modern life. In commerce, manufacturers and retailers alike protect their sources, their suppliers, by developing cordial relations or writing intricate legal contracts or vertically integrating ownership, because they know how vulnerable they are if supplies don't arrive. Similarly, in economic development, governments build infrastructure—roads, communications, power—as the springboard from which industry and retail can launch. What is upstream, economically speaking, is precious, essential to protect.

If the sources of manufacturing, retailing, and economic development are self-evidently in need of protection, then, in an ecologically sustainable world, so too are *natural sources*, the water and soil and atmosphere that are the logical and ultimate upstream origin of all that is human-made. But, unlike most economic sources, natural sources are the ultimate material sources. They have no substitutes, they can be irretrievably lost, and so they must be absolutely protected: *biophysical ultimates require social absolutes*.

Spiritually speaking, ultimate sources are sacred. To sacrifice an ultimate resource is a sacrilege. In contrast, to sacrifice the *benefits* otherwise derived from using up an ultimate source—to refrain from stripping topsoil, from draining an aquifer, from driving an organism to extinction, from opening the ozone layer, all for commercial gain—to sacrifice these benefits is to *elevate* human action. It is to reach the highest form of restraint in humans' material relations, to find humans' place in nature. Or, as Wendell Berry puts it, it is to preserve the ends in the means. It is to achieve purpose in life, to connect with the larger world, to gain meaning by protecting the means to the good life, especially the ultimate means which, in the material, ecological world are sources.

Recall from the preface that Edward Abbey saw no shortage of water in the desert. We might go on to say that if there is any shortage, it is in our ability to live within our means on this one and only planet. It is there that we must adapt to the fluctuations of nature. It is there that we need to find enough, and not too much. It is there that we have to accept that some things have no place among living things and should be capped or banned. And it is there that ultimate sources cannot be sacrificed, precisely because they are irreplaceable and sacred and should be treated as such.

Intermittency, sufficiency, capping, and sourcing may appear unduly demanding, but probably no more so than the demands on those who created a nation or promoted industrialization or fought for abolition and against totalitarianism. Certainly these principles are at least as sensible as the observation that there is just the right amount of water in the desert. This is because these principles are aimed at *fit*—at fitting human's material system, its "economy," to the requisites of Planet Earth, not the other way around. They all embrace a notion of limits, just as the earth and its inhabitants and its cycles of water and nutrients and seasons exhibit limits. And while they may apply at any scale—local, regional, national, international—they aim at place, at the very foundations of an economy. These principles thus lay primary groundwork for a home economy, from the local to the global. Next is practice, doing good work, connecting natural and social systems.

6

The Elm Stand

At my office I have a keyboard stand made of American elm. I made it myself, from one-and-a-half-inch planks I dried, planed, edged, ripsawed, crosscut, routed, scraped, and sanded. Its four pieces fit together without nails or screws, only with dovetail joints and glue. Once the stand was assembled, I finished the wood with tung oil, hand-rubbing it and allowing each coat to dry for several days before sanding. Repeating the process a half dozen times brought out the full richness of the grain and at the same time added a patina to the wood's surface. Finally, I applied three coats of wax, hand-rubbing and polishing each coat till the surface fairly gleamed.

It would never win a prize or a spot in a woodworker's magazine. But I see it as quite a piece of work because it is *my* work, and work that, I only realized some time later, connects my everyday practice—writing—to a once-living thing. It turns out that it is also the work of many others, some going back, I surmise, a century or more. Some university landscaper probably planted the sapling knowing that over the years it would take the classic vase shape of the American elm. No doubt he also knew that he would never see it in such magnificence, but he planted it anyway. It was his work, and through that work he created value. In fact, all of us involved with this tree created value. For me, though, the story goes back some fifteen years.

One bright spring day I was walking my five-year-old son across campus after day care when we came upon a yellow caution ribbon. Behind the ribbon a university tree-cutting crew was preparing to take down a giant elm. Quite a crowd had gathered. We stopped to watch.

The crew had secured ropes high up on the trunk to keep it from falling on a nearby building—my own office building, actually, the University of Michigan's School of Natural Resources and Environment. The crew told everyone to stand back as the chainsaw operator, a burly man with a confident swagger, approached the base of the tree.

He wore a sleeveless T-shirt, probably to show off his ample biceps. His chest puffed out and his muscles became taught as he revved up the chain saw. He exuded power. I detected a sense of anticipation, of a major event, on his face. Having cut down a few trees myself, I knew the feeling. Whatever one thinks about trees and logging, felling a tree, especially one this big, is a thrill. And this guy had an audience to boot.

In no time he cut a wedge out of the base, the others tugged on the ropes, and down it came. My son's jaw dropped, his eyes opened wide. My heart raced. I could imagine, in fact, I could *feel* the rush the chainsaw operator must have felt. What a spectacle!

So that was that. Another elm tree bites the dust, no doubt another victim of Dutch elm disease, which has ravaged American elms across North America for decades and nearly driven them to extinction. My son went home with my wife, and I entered the Dana Building (named after Samuel Trask Dana, one of the country's early scientific foresters). I sat in my office trying to work while listening to the chainsaw and chipper make short work of the elm's carcass.

What a shame, I thought. All that wood just cut up and ground up, destined most likely for a landfill somewhere. I couldn't sit still, so I went back out. Only the trunk was left, some ten feet long and two and a half to three feet in diameter. The chainsaw operator was about to chop it into blocks. I approached him.

"You going to cut this up?"

"Yup. Gotta get it out before the end of the day."

"It's elm, right?"

"Yeah."

"Wouldn't it make good lumber?"

"I suppose so. I just gotta get it out of here."

"Kind of a waste."

He shrugged. I turned to go, not wanting to interfere anymore with this guy, who was just doing his job and who, I guessed, did not appreciate being questioned by some tree hugger from the environment school. But then he cleared his throat and spoke.

"Cutting this tree *was* a waste."

"What?"

"This tree didn't have to come down."

"It was diseased, wasn't it?"

"No. Perfectly healthy."

"But why would—"

"They're putting in a sidewalk with a short wall. The wall requires a footer, below the frost line. That'd cut off almost half the tree's roots. Eventually it'd fall. So they ordered me to take it down. I fought it all summer, but I lost."

I just looked at him. His eyes welled and I could see he was choking up.

"I lost a friend today." He turned away.

We just stood there. Somehow we got to talking about elm wood and how rare it is and how, with proper milling and curing, it can be made into some very nice furniture. Before I knew it, I was asking to take the trunk and do just that. He agreed, as long as I got it out by the end of the day. Having ridden my bike that day, I was in a bit of a bind. But in short order a couple of loggers were hauling the trunk off campus and to a nearby mill.

Several weeks later I got a call from the sawyer at the mill. "This wood is beautiful! I've never seen anything like it. Every cut is different—brown, blonde, red. You got yourself some good wood there!" I was proud. He called again in a few days and said it was ready to pick up, all cut into one-and-a-half- and two-and-a-half-inch planks. After letting the wood dry in the campus woodshop for two or three years, I began making my elm stand.

Reconnection

If there were a single philosophical position in environmental thought, adhered to by all who are concerned about environmental destruction, it is that at the root of that destruction is humans' separation from nature. Perhaps it sounds like a cliché, but that separation, that condition of "man apart from nature," of alienation from the natural world, of distancing, is what drives overharvesting, overconsuming, overpumping, overdumping, and all the other excesses of modern industrial life, amply documented in a multitude of state-of-the-environment reports. All this disconnection is spurred by mechanization, commodification, commercialization, urbanization, long-distance transport, packaging, central heating and cooling, electronic communication, formal education, reading, touring, zoos, and, well, just about every product and process that constitutes modern life. What all of them do is promote consumption, mobility, speed, entertainment, health (or, maybe better, longevity), information. And, of course, they promote growth, endlessly increasing throughput of material and energy in humans' subsystem, what one might call its "economy," of that larger system, what one might call the biosphere. At the same time, they skew perceptions away from the biophysical basis of economic activity, indeed, from the material basis of human life.

The obvious mechanisms of separation are physical—the lack of direct contact with natural processes. Milk comes from cartons, paper from a box, gasoline from a pump. Drinking water flows from the tap, food from the grocery store. Less obvious but perhaps equally important are the concepts and technologies that drive a modern society. We don't see the cow that produces the milk, let alone the farm, but we don't need to: markets for feed and feedlots, for dairy products and packaging, for trucking and shelving all ensure supply. Milk is always available; just plunk down the cash. Concepts like "supply and demand" and "efficient production" and "food safety" join with actual distribution and financing systems to make it all happen. Consumers needn't worry their pretty heads over where it comes from or what it looks like along the way or what goes in and what comes out in the process. Be a good consumer, we're enjoined—just buy, and then buy some more.

If separation from nature drives excess natural resource use, then connection would do the reverse. For many observers, this means people should better appreciate nature, and for that they need environmental education. But studying an environmental text (present author's excluded, of course) or watching a nature program or spending time "in nature," let alone spending money on "natural products," tends, in a commercial society, to just reinforce a consumerist approach—buy it, use it up, go on to the next thing. Should it somehow result from educational measures, a heightened consciousness of nature is primarily about individual uplift and redemption, not about changing a society's relationship with natural processes. Because "the

environment" responds to total extraction and total waste filling—not to activities at the margin, not to individual action—
these measures do little, if anything, to arrest the trends. They
do little to find a new path; instead, they ease the burden as we
tread heavily up that ever more precarious ridge.

A societal shift in consciousness—in practical terms, a shift
in social norms and organizing principles—thus requires more
than enhanced "environmental awareness." It requires three
things: (1) modes of *practice* enabled by a language of connection and by organization for connection; (2) a rich notion of
work, not just a job but productive engagement; and (3) a diverse or pluralist concept of *value*, not market value but value
that is at once human and natural. To explore these features of
a home economy in an ecological order, let's return to the elm
tree and, in particular, to the chainsaw operator.

Apart?

Was the chainsaw operator a man apart from nature, or was he
a man of nature, connected to its functionings, some known,
some mysterious? Or was he just a guy doing a job?

At first glance, he was just taking orders and getting the job
done—the job as defined by his superiors, apparently. He put
in his hours and collected his paycheck. And what he did was
cut trees, and probably plant a few, too.

On closer examination, it is clear (to this observer, anyway)
that in this instance he sized up the situation, the planned sidewalk with a knee-high wall, and took a stance, a moral stance.
Yes, he cut trees day after day (the city crew cuts, on average,
some ten or twelve trees a day in season), but we can surmise
that he cut trees that were diseased or too old to stand much
longer or that were storm-damaged. He did not cut, as a rule,
perfectly healthy trees, and certainly did not cut mature Ameri-

can elms, the very species the university had invested untold funds trying to save.

Trees were his business, to be sure, but a business that treats trees right, with care, with judiciousness. You cut them when you have to, not on a whim, not to make a few extra dollars. And certainly not to widen a sidewalk and build a short wall.

He called the elm tree his "friend," an apt metaphor. Friendships develop over time. They require intimate knowledge, and at times they are demanding; they may even require sacrifice. But they also require care and protection, what this tree no doubt offered to many squirrels, birds, and insects, and to not a few students and professors in its century of life, and what this gentleman offered the tree through a summer of protest. Friendships also require letting go, what this gentleman did time and again, whenever his chainsaw sank into a tree on the first cut.

So in this case and in these various ways—care, judicious cutting, intimate knowledge, protection, letting go—the chainsaw operator was indeed connected. He was connected through practice, through engaged work, not through education and lecturing, what had been occurring for decades only steps away from that very tree.

In the larger scheme of things, this case is trivial. The tree was not part of a natural forest. Urban foresters cut trees, including healthy ones, all the time. Nevertheless, this case might just tell us something about the possibility of a tighter human connection to nature in other settings, even in the broader political economy. The mechanism is the language of value, what is routinely taken in a commercial society to be market value, or in industrial development the value of progress (every advance is presumed beneficial until proven otherwise), yet in an ecological society can be—and, arguably, must be—much more.

Value in Ecological Order

Before we make important decisions, it is a commonplace in so-called advanced industrial societies to ask how much a thing is worth. Only then can we act: that is, act rationally, sensibly, with full consideration of the opportunity costs and the value of our time and the money we could earn. This question is applied everywhere, from fire insurance to classroom size to roadway safety to species extinction to climate disruption: How much will it cost? Will the economy be hurt?

So what is the "value" of my elm stand? I might get ten or twenty dollars at a garage sale. Is that its value? I might burn it in a fireplace for an hour. Is that its value? Or maybe I could calculate the material and labor costs of rerouting that sidewalk or forgoing the knee-high wall and its footing. Then I would have the true value. Or so many people seem to believe—people in positions of power and influence, people who say we can't afford to insure the vulnerable, can't afford to lower school class size, or slow traffic to protect pedestrians and save gas, or slow the economy out of concern over a warming climate.

To accept such an assignment of value is to denigrate all that the elm stand has meant to me, to the people who know its story, and to the sawyer, the chainsaw operator, and the landscapers who nurtured it for a century of life, not to mention those who once sat in its shade and admired its classic vase shape. And what of the fact that this particular tree actually survived Dutch elm disease, even when trees all around it succumbed? Isn't there some "value" in that?

In an ecological era these questions would hardly need asking. Of course there is great value, multiple values, in that tree. And, notice, I am not referring to "the value of nature," value independent of human action. Recall that the elm tree's environment was human-made. I am talking here about those values that are *dependent* on human action (or inaction) at the same time that human action is dependent on nature, as it always is. The elm required human care, but we users were required by the elm to care for it and its environment in ways that respected natural processes. I sensed that the chainsaw operator knew this, even if the university planners did not.

In the end, then, it is the *inter*dependency via work and a rich notion of value that connects humans to nature. This is how reconnection takes place, not through nature study and paying extra for a bit of green. So let's take the consideration of value a step further.

In the elm case, by all appearances (short of the conversation he and I had), the university was just "developing" its resources, clearing the way for a much-needed path between buildings. The intended benefit was enhanced accessibility and mobility for users—students, professors, staff, grounds crew. The cost was one less tree and some work and materials. Benefits presumably exceeded costs, so the project went forward. Overall value from the operation went up.

At the same time, though, a different calculus was being made by the chainsaw operator, by me, and by whomever else was moved by this tree's demise and its eventual configuration as lumber and furniture (one thick plank is a mantle above a friend's fireplace). For us, value lodged first and foremost in the tree itself, the *living* tree, the organism that offered shade and habitat, that stood tall and looked right on a campus quad, that somehow escaped the ravages of Dutch elm disease and thus might have harbored genetic traits useful in reestablishing the American elm. Value for us also lodged in the work performed for that tree, from its initial planting to its final joining and polishing.

Implicit in both valuations, the tree itself and the human care, is a much deeper value, one hard to express yet central to an ecological order. Two useful starting points, though, are thermodynamics and ecological integrity. From a strictly thermodynamic perspective, value inheres in an item whenever entropy is lowered, when order increases, when high-quality energy enters a system and that system resists dissipation by self-organizing.[1] Photosynthesis combines high entropy H_2O and CO_2 to form low-entropy cellulose. The tree grows, and when growth ceases, it maintains itself. Moreover, the ecological component of this "value added," that is, the *systems* component, is the dependence of such low entropy on a complex set of functions supplied not just by the tree but by the tree's original forest ecosystem. The ecosystem's ability to create low-entropy cellulose over the long term depends on its integrity as a forest ecosystem. Such integrity includes the ability to adapt to disturbance without flipping irreversibly into a simpler degraded system, as when cutover forests on weak soils convert to scrubland without forest regeneration.[2]

So the value of low-entropy material such as wood depends in part on an *organism's functioning* (a tree photosynthesizing) and in part on that particular *ecosystem's functioning* (the forest components interacting, creating and storing and transmitting information, all working as a complex, high-integrity adaptive system). The true, ecologically nuanced value of a resource is, first, that derived from ecosystem functioning and, second, that derived from human application. What's more, every resource is to some extent uniquely constituted by the particular combination of the ecosystem and the human application.

Thus, the elm seedling or its progenitors ultimately came from a forest, a "wild" place that evolved over thousands of years, adapting constantly to its place. That place and that adapting may have included humans who were, say, clearing and burning and selecting tree species. What the seedling contained was all the evolved information of its lineage. That information (and, once again, this idea is hard to express because the term *information* seems so neutral, so devoid of life) cannot be cataloged, counted, let alone "valued" in the marketplace or chalked up as "development." And it cannot be replaced. It is invaluable; that is, its value is incalculable. So no trade-off function can be constructed, no benefit-cost ratio written, no exchange rate established. It is precious, indeed, sacred. To sacrifice that tree and all its embodied information is a sacrilege. To sacrifice the width of the sidewalk and the construction of the wall, from this perspective, is the obvious thing to do (see chapter 7).

In other words, what exists in my elm stand is an elm stand of a different sort, elms in an ancient forest, evolved, adapted, with a good fit. Its value is every bit as real (witness the reactions of us observers and participants) as any other value, including those that get dollar signs attached. Its value is there, and I have little doubt that the gentleman with the chainsaw sensed it, intensely, just as I sense it every time I rest my palms on the stand to type. It is precious.

In an ecological order, such values must be front and center, and because this "trivial" case demonstrates their existence and potential, they can be. With fundamental societal shifts under way, the values of "development" or of the market or of the newest technology or the "next big thing" in consumer items no longer merit the deference they have been shown. What merits deference is that which reaches far back in time, through evolved adaptations, and far into the future, in anticipation of new adaptations. Something as simple and mundane as a wood stand for a keyboard suggests that such Janus-faced temporal gazing is easier than one might think. It also suggests that a long time horizon, an essential ingredient in an ecological order, is unlikely to be found in the fleeting artifacts of human technological cleverness—the keyboard and computer itself, say, not to mention the data and messages they transmit.

Rather, a long time horizon is to be found where humans directly engage nature in productive enterprise, where the saw strikes the tree, the plane shaves the board, and, elsewhere, where the plow tills the soil, the net catches the fish, the pump delivers the water. In other words, it is where work is performed—not just any work, but, rather, the work that connects and has meaning beyond the assigned tasks and the paycheck and the items that can be purchased with that paycheck. It is where care and concern, protection and nurturing come naturally, regardless of price or technological sophistication or fame or fortune.

This is the kind of value that connects and that already exists, no matter how overshadowed and denigrated it is by industrial, commercial, and consumerist values. This is value that, because it does exist, can be highlighted, even elevated above the industrial, commercial, and consumerist. This is the value that we take as given when the goal is *living with nature for a long time*, when the goal is fitting human activity, especially its economy, into this one and only planet. Its expression can be as simple as saving a tree from "development" or making furniture from a precious piece of wood. Its organization can be as straightforward as building an economy that is actually *economical*—our next topic.

7

Beyond the Consumer Economy

The *American Heritage Dictionary* defines economical as "prudent and thrifty in management; not wasteful or extravagant."[1] So what might an *economical economy* be? What might an economy be that is prudent in its use of renewable resources such as forests, grasslands, and water, and thrifty in its use of nonrenewable resources such as oil, coal, and minerals? What might an economy be that avoids creating wastes society does not want and cannot handle?

In the current freewheeling economy, the one deliberately designed to create new markets and pry open old ones, to relax regulations and abolish traditional practices, to subsidize energy sources and lower prices (even if some costs are only displaced, not paid), in this economy it is hard to imagine. Yet if an economy is not economical, what kind of thing is it? For starters, I argue in this chapter, it is a mining and consuming economy. It is both an extractive machine on an endless frontier and a beast of no burdens on an extravagant shopping spree.

The central point in this chapter is that there are many economies. Some are nested within other economies (the household economy is part of the larger market economy, for example), and some exist at the periphery (the hunting and foraging economy, for instance). Each economy serves a purpose. But not all contribute to a home economy, let alone to ecological order.

For the purpose of structuring resource use so as to live within our means, we need an economical economy. We need an economy organized not only around principles like intermittency, sufficiency, capping, and sourcing (chapter 5), but also around virtues like prudence and thrift. Such an economy would embody through its resource use an *ethic of living on this one and only planet*.

A Mining Economy

A mining economy takes as axiomatic that resources are to be used and, when a rational calculation can be made, used up. It explores, tests, extracts, manufactures, distributes, consumes, throws away, then goes back for more. When the stuff is all gone, it goes elsewhere, to new frontiers where raw materials and places to dump abound. What it leaves behind is waste. In fact, a mining economy creates waste, unlike nature's economy where, in ecological communities, one organism's excretion is another's nutrient. Creating waste for which there is no use is one defining feature of this uneconomical economy.

Another defining feature is its intellectual pedigree. Behind it all is a form of reasoning, an analytic framework, a set of sophisticated models. It is called neoclassical economics, within which resource economics starts with a simple premise: there is an optimal extraction rate for every resource. "Optimal" refers to that which generates the most benefit over a given time period—in practice, a time period relevant to investors and politicians. And in practice, "benefit" usually means money, private or public. It makes little difference whether the resource is oil (the exemplar for most models) or timber (let alone forests) or water (which can be locally depleted) or fish (which move around a lot and whose populations look normal until they crash).

In this framework, the optimal extraction rate is a function of consumer demand, interest rates, and available technologies, none of which have ecological content. The presumed goal is to maximize benefits (for example, revenues, appropriations, return on investment, profit, market share) over a chosen time period (that is, a period chosen by those who want returns now, or in a few months or years). For oil the extraction rate is adjusted as demand, interest rates, technologies, and the political environment change, but eventually the oil is, of course, depleted. Yet timber is modeled in largely the same way, and as a result, it often makes sense (rational, economistic sense) to clear old-growth forests and plant monoculture plantations. It's all about depletion, optimal depletion.

Perhaps the most telling concept in this entire intellectual architecture is "optimal extinction." The reasoning, once again, is no different from that of oil and forests: a useful species (whales are the exemplar in such analyses) should be completely harvested and the proceeds invested whenever the returns on such investments exceed the benefits of keeping the species.

In short, this is an economics of depletion, of mining. It undergirds much decision making in business and in public policy making, domestic and international. It assumes depletion as a natural state of affairs, self-evident for minerals and equally rational for all other resources, no matter how renewable, how essential to life, how integral to ecosystem functioning or climate stability. This thinking acts as if there will always be more resources, another forest to clear, another fishery to fish, another aquifer to pump. Or it assumes that technology will find substitutes. It is inherently expansionist. It is a fundamental way of thinking and, consequently, of decision making and policy making. It is a major contributor to current patterns of ecological decline. It rationalizes and legitimates a mining economy when a sustaining economy is possible. It is inherently uneconomical, wasteful of all that is, or could be, renewing and life-supporting.

So a mining economy tends to mine all: minerals, oil, soil, forests, aquifers. It decapitates mountaintops for coal, depletes freshwater aquifers for cattle feed, and fills the oceans and atmosphere with climate-disrupting substances to "keep the economy going." Along the way, it tends to mine families and communities of their self-help, their productive capacities, their ability to self-provision. It requires people to assume as their primary economic role that of consumer, buying more and more so as to be the "engine of economic growth."

A Consuming Economy

A mining economy uses up and throws away; it *consumes*. But in so-called advanced industrial economies, a mining economy is also consumer*ist*. A farmer who buys fertilizers and herbicides to maximize yields, who buys machines and the fuel to run them, who hires labor and pays them a wage, all because the scale of operation is too big to do otherwise, is running a consumerist enterprise. It is more than coincidental that such enterprises also tend to consume the soil and water and biota that surround them. And it is probably more than coincidental that farming communities disappear as these enterprises consolidate their holdings. By the same token, a householder who hires plumbers and carpenters and cleaners for every household task (what would otherwise be called a "chore") who eats out, who drives everywhere, even the corner store, is running a consumerist household. The consumer can respond only to price and hence can be responsible for very little else, certainly not the quality of the soil and water or the standards of labor. The ethics of consumerism is the ethics of smart shopping, getting good deals, employing others, and substituting technology for disciplined work and care. The consumer is thus burdened by little more than continuous shopping and hiring.

A home economy, by contrast, generates and regenerates; it is self-sustaining. Its roots are *producerist* (chapter 9), not consumerist. People are defined not by their shopping but by their producing, by their ability to buy as little as possible. Its burdens are more substantial—making, creating, caring—and its responsibilities closer to home—wastes either assimilate or are prevented altogether.

In value terms (chapter 6), to emphasize buying is to value ephemeral relationships, relationships with little attachment, little obligation, little allegiance beyond that prescribed in a contract or through the exchange of money. To imagine that a consumerist economy could be sustainable is to believe that there is "good consuming" and "bad consuming" and that all that is needed is more of the good, less of the bad. In fact, all consuming is using up. Some, of course, is necessary for life. But the great bulk of consuming in modern industrial consumer economies is "for the economy." If there is caring in this economy, it is care *for the economy*, not for its members; it is care for abstract measures like GDP and stock market indexes and the shareholder value of absentee owners, not for the resource base on which it rests, not for the actual work on the ground that keeps it all going.

An economical economy, therefore, does not arise when its consumption patterns simply become greener and more environmentally friendly. Rather, an economical economy puts consumption in its proper place, meeting basic material needs, and puts production in its proper place, meeting basic human needs for making, creating, and caring. In its highest forms, the practices of an economical economy, its "productiveness"—that very making, creating, and caring—are *disciplines*, even *arts*. Unlike the practices of the consumer economy, where relevant decisions (consumer decisions) are binary—buy or not buy—the practices of a producer economy lie along a continuum of decisions, each with varying opportunities and responsibilities. At one end are the simple productive acts—boiling an egg, pulling a weed, writing a letter. At the other end are the disciplines, the spiritual, and the arts. In Michael Ende's children's story about time, *Momo*, Beppo Roadsweeper is a simple, kind man who does his work, sweeping roads. But he doesn't just punch a clock and put in his hours. His work is "a useful job, and he knows it." So he does the job right, as a discipline:

He swept his allotted streets slowly but steadily, drawing a deep breath before every step and every stroke of the broom. Step, breathe, sweep, step, breathe, sweep. . . . Every so often he would pause awhile, staring thoughtfully into the distance. And then he would begin again: step, breathe, sweep. . . .

While progressing in this way, with a dirty street ahead of him and a clean one behind, he often had grand ideas. They were ideas that couldn't easily be put into words, though—ideas as hard to define as a half-remembered scent or a color seen in a dream. . . .

"Sometimes, when you've a very long street ahead of you," [Beppo explained,] "you think how terribly long it is and feel sure you'll never get it swept. . . . And then you start to hurry. . . . You work faster and faster, and every time you look up there seems to be just as much left to sweep as before, and you try even harder, and you panic, and in the end you're out of breath and have to stop—and still the street stretches away in front of you. That's not the way to do it."

"You must never think of the whole street at once, understand? You must only concentrate on the next step, the next breath, the next stroke of the broom, and the next, and the next. Nothing else."

"That way you enjoy your work, which is important, because then you make a good job of it. And that's how it ought to be."

"And all at once, before you know it, you find you've swept the whole street clean, bit by bit. What's more, you aren't out of breath. . . . That's important, too."[2]

Farmer and social critic Wendell Berry also sees in disciplined work the bridging of competing tendencies of the practical and the spiritual. But he cautions against seeing spirituality as the antidote to the modern dilemma:

Now that the practical processes of industrial civilization have become so threatening to humanity and to nature, it is easy for us, or for some of us, to see that practicality needs to be made subject to spiritual values and spiritual measures. But we must not forget that it is also necessary for spirituality to be responsive to practical questions. For human beings the spiritual and the practical are, and should be, inseparable. Alone, practicality becomes dangerous; spirituality, alone, becomes feeble and pointless. Alone, either becomes dull. Each is the other's discipline, in a sense, and in good work, the two are joined.[3]

So how would good work help create an economical economy? How would one even begin to craft such an economy? As the trekkers discovered, a good place to start is with what exists. If it exists, it is possible. Other economies have existed, and other economies do exist; in fact, they are all around us. There are the household economy, the community economy, the economies of care (for children, the elderly, and the infirm, on the one hand, and farms, landscapes, art, and artifacts of cultural significance, on the other). And, of course, there is nature's economy. These warrant the term *economy* as much as the dominant one, the mining and consuming economy. These economies are also systems of exchange, of material flow, of value; they just do not have the same metrics as the dominant economy, let alone the same values. They do not fit into neat equations or align along supply and demand curves, let alone macroeconomic trajectories of endless growth. Instead, these "other economies" conjoin the practical and the spiritual. Unlike the consumerist, industrial economy, they are economical of people and place, of culture and agriculture, of human nature and nature's nature. And they appear to exhibit a common set of principles and virtues.

A Producer Economy

We probably know enough about the consumer economy. Its theorists—economists—are the high priests of a modern industrial society. Its advocates span the ideological spectrum, from conservative and pro-business to liberal and pro-labor, yet all pro-growth. Its critics have charged that it is too materialistic (e.g., too much shopping), not materialistic enough (e.g., too little appreciation of handiwork), insensitive to external impacts (upstream and down), and that, in combination with population and technology, it drives widespread environmental change.

Assume the consumer economy has had its run, that it is deeply implicated in humanity's (primarily the North's) excess throughput of material and energy, abundantly documented in one report after another. Assume that the mindset of "the consumer" is fundamentally demeaning, that the construction of the "sovereign consumer" is an all too convenient excuse for powerful actors to evade their societal and environmental responsibilities (chapter 3). With just these two assumptions, it is clearly time for a change, time to shift to a home economy. A useful starting point would be a consumer economy's apparent polar opposite, a "producer economy."

To begin to imagine a "producer economy," try this thought experiment, an exercise in turning the tables (or maybe in turning the tide from endless flow to ebb and flow).[4]

A consumer economy, we have seen, is inherently a mining economy—it's all about using and using up. Everyone is, first and foremost, a consumer. Consumers decide what gets produced, used, and thrown away. Consumption drives the economy. To reverse things, everyone is a producer in a producer economy, in the sense of making, creating, and caring for. One does not "sell one's labor"; one self-produces. Self-production means that each individual or self-organized group or self-governed community would decide what is produced. Like producers everywhere, human and nonhuman, they would produce useful things and they would produce waste. Furthermore, these very producers would decide what is waste and how *they*, not others, will live with it.

A fanciful idea? Perhaps. But consider that it was little more than a century ago in the United States that much of the economy was so organized, led by artisans, skilled craftspeople, small shop owners, independent yeoman farmers and tinkers, inventors of the very technologies that spurred industrialization. To be sure, businesspeople were committed to making products, selling them, and earning a profit. But they were equally committed to the notion that political independence was inextricably intertwined with economic independence and the integrity of one's immediate community. Democracy depended on a populace that could produce for itself, not just at the national level but at the level of the individual, the household, and the immediate community. "Freedom could not flourish in a nation of hirelings," wrote historian and social critic Christopher Lasch.[5] Nor, one might add from a more recent vantage point, could a rich, democratic type of freedom flourish in a nation of consumers. Back then, small proprietors in the United States, as well as in England and France, resisted the label "working class," seeing themselves instead as *producers*, people who identified their enemy not as employers (they were self-employed, after all) but as parasitic bankers, speculators, monopolists, and middlemen (chapter 9).

Still fanciful? Now try this thought experiment. Imagine that a century or so ago, at a time of extensive self-production, someone came along and proposed a consumer economy. Only rather than selling the idea as the way to feed one's family or get rich or be modern (the most persuasive selling point of all), the booster sold it for what it would actually become—a means of alienating work and enriching owners, of pursuing fleeting pleasures with objects soon to become obsolete, of breaking up the family and community, of becoming dependent on mobile capital, of accumulating debt (for self and nation), of mining resources, even the renewable ones, and filling waste sinks, even the regenerative ones. (Admittedly, this would be an odd sort of booster as, by definition, boosters highlight the positive and shade the negative. But this is a thought experiment!) Would this society go for it? Would it leave its rewarding, productive path for a consuming path? Hard to imagine. Instead, self-producers would take advantage of technological advances whenever they advanced self-production, but not when they replaced self-production with wage work and shopping, with being a "consumer"—a strange beast if there ever was one.

Whether a producer economy could have happened or, back then, *should* have happened is beside the point. Now a consumer economy reigns supreme, and it does not work—not for the so-called consumer, not for workers, not for citizens, and not for the planet. It is self-destructive. A producer economy, by contrast, could be self-productive. Its measure would be not the output of consumables (so-called goods even when they include oil spill cleanups and hospital visits) but its near opposite—the extent to which consumables are unnecessary. Just as insulation in attics makes a power plant outside town unnecessary, self-producing makes much consuming unnecessary.

To illustrate, imagine a neighborhood with carpenters, plumbers, landscapers, doctors, and fruit and vegetable growers. With a bit of organization, they could provision themselves with much of their basic needs. In so doing, their overall consumption, their draw on natural resources, and their disposing of wastes would be far lower than when such services are distanced (their production and end use separated by geography or middlemen or cultural divides or power differences) and contracted out.[6] In fact, a neighbor of mine has done just this. He and some friends created a "time bank." Members request services and offer their own. Each hour of service rendered is credited at the bank and can be drawn on for services needed. No money exchanged (beyond necessary purchases), and very little transport—it's all in the neighborhood.

As the time bank suggests, a producer economy is inherently democratic and egalitarian. It minimizes money exchange and maximizes interpersonal exchange. A core organizing principle is self-ownership and community ownership. That is, patterns of ownership tend to match patterns of production. The local potter has her own wheel, the potters' guild collectively owns the kiln, and the city operates a public arts and crafts market.

In addition to being democratic, a producer economy is more likely to achieve what market enthusiasts claim: namely, high levels of satisfaction. But that satisfaction would come from good work, not good shopping. Think about the work of all those associated with the elm tree in chapter 6. And, as we will see in chapter 9, consider the fact that there is a wealth of literature, from the social scientific to the literary, that supports the notion that meaning and hope come from engagement, productive engagement, not from buying, not from taking orders and seeking convenience, comfort, and entertainment.

A producer economy is a working economy. Its goal is good work, not output, not GDP, and certainly not a GDP that must increase every year, forever, by mining everything from oil and soil to families and communities. A producer economy makes little sense when the purpose is rapid frontier exploitation and when mining is unproblematic. But it makes great sense when the purpose is to maintain fundamental life-support systems, when preparation and prevention and precaution are the bywords, when, in short, *prudence* and *thrift* are highly valued. This would be the case when a society's risks proliferate beyond control, when cheap fossil fuels no longer propel a global whirlwind of commercialization, when the only thing hold-ing up the financial system is "confidence": in short, when the economy is a house of cards, not a home economy.

Principles, values, virtues, ethics. Here in part II we have laid some groundwork and assembled some scaffolding for con-structing an ecological order. Now we need tools, by which I mean devices for framing problems. Framing problems, after all, is the requisite first step toward solving problems. Part III begins with a positive notion of sacrifice and the idea of limits and well-being through work. It then picks up language and worldview, finishing with levers for hopeful change. These are tools for building a material order that is at once ecological and ethical, that extends a time horizon to the very long term. They are straightforward, yet difficult.

The difficulty lies, once again, not in the complexity of the task but in how problems have been framed, in the worldviews that have, for a century or more, been fabulously successful: successful in producing and consuming goods, where goods are good and more goods are presumed better, all as if there are no serious bads; successful in conflating those goods with the good life. A new success for a new normal, beyond the consumer economy, is now in order.

III

Tools for an Ecological Order

8

It Isn't Easy

According to one of the great authorities on global affairs, it isn't easy saving the environment. Kermit the Frog is having an adventure in the great, green outdoors, singing, "It's not that easy being green." He comes to a clearing in the forest. There stands a big, shiny, brand-new Ford Escape Hybrid sport utility vehicle. He looks it over carefully. On the back side he sees a decal: "Hybrid," it reads.

"Huh! I guess it *is* easy being green!"[1]

There is a part of me that wants to believe Kermit the Frog. I would guess nearly everyone else who is concerned about the global environmental crisis does too. We want to ignore his corporate sponsors and clever marketers and just go along with the ride: a little retooling here, an efficiency there, a catchy tune and, presto, all's well. Would that it were so.

But it is not. To say it is not, though, is not to say all is bad, that all is a steady decline into the abyss of poverty and misery, a walk out of Kermit's bright, leafy Shangri-La into a cold, dark cave. Surprisingly enough, a useful device for seeing a bright future, a future with less consuming and more producing, less buying and more making and creating and caring (chapter 7), is an old-fashioned, much-invoked, and much-maligned term: *sacrifice.*[2]

Current Sacrifice

I know we're consuming too much. But if we cut back, the economy will take a dive. People will lose their jobs. Public services will decline. Democracy will be put at risk. And besides, people just won't make the sacrifice. Why should they?

Every time I speak about overconsumption, this is the kind of question I get.[3] A newspaper editor once asked me to write a piece on how we can reduce consumption without hurting the economy. I have tried, but it is always a struggle, and I have yet to come up with a convincing reply (see, though, chapter 4). Dealing with the charge of sacrifice, with the call for moderns to turn off the lights, crawl into the cave, and shiver in the dark, is a perennial problem in my work, one I would just as soon dodge (and have dodged on many an occasion). Yet in the face of ever-increasing use of resources and filling of waste sinks, sacrifice may be the crucial issue: if consuming less entails sacrifice, including the sacrifice of our very way of life and livelihood, how can a society possibly save the environment? If we take "the environment" as our life-support system, at once adaptive and fragile, how can we save ourselves?

This is indeed an important question, maybe the essential question in the face of excess throughput and its attendant impacts, environmental and human. It is the right question. And it is the wrong question.

It is the right question in part because it forces all would-be environmental saviors (this author included) to confront their prescriptions. If one has moved from marginal change—"diddling with details," as systems analyst Donella Meadows called it—to fundamental restructuring, one can hardly avoid concluding that the economy must change. But in a consumption-driven economy, to say we must restructure and reduce consumption is to invite disaster, and from this perspective it is the wrong question. It is wrong because it requires that we accept at face value the prevailing framing of sacrifice. Let's do a bit of reframing.

The reluctance to engage sacrifice, to accept sacrifice as a worthy approach to righting environmental wrongs, presumes that society is not *already* sacrificing to pursue the status quo. Yet every day in the United States we sacrifice about one hundred people on the highways (plus ten to fifteen times that number of people seriously injured). Day after day, year in and year out. A 9/11 tragedy every month. And we hardly blink. All to pursue a particular value expressed with a particular kind of vehicle—personal mobility via an automobile. Society's endorsement of this sacrifice is evidenced by the huge public investment for automobile infrastructure and the reluctance to slow traffic and protect pedestrians (a significant fraction of deaths and injuries are to nonmotorists). If just one person died every day from airline or railroad accidents, let alone from a new disease, there would be a public outcry. Less obvious (perhaps) is the military expense and lives lost to protect oil supplies. And in our commitment to market-based, consumer-led health care in the United States, we sacrifice eighteen thousand lives annually for lack of health insurance.[4] And now, as one report after another confirms the disruptive effects of global warming, we appear to be in the middle of a long-term project to sacrifice vast coastal areas, mangroves, coral reefs, and cropland, even entire nations, all to maintain a carbon-based economy. The list goes on. These are signs of a sacrificial consumer economy. Modern industrial societies are making huge sacrifices to pursue a particular vision of the good life.

These forms of sacrifice are well documented but known, it seems, only to the specialist and the well-informed citizen. Nobody is hiding them, yet they are effectively covert, hidden from view or scrutiny because they are treated as anomalies, as problems that just need fixing. They are, the reasoning appears to go, aberrations that, with the will (especially political will) and the money (especially public money) can be solved (chapter 4). In fact, if we rev up the economy, do more of what we are already doing but with, say, better cars (e.g., Kermit's hybrid SUV) and more renewables in the fuel mix (even if we end up just doing more of what we are currently doing), we can generate the wealth, the surplus revenues, to tackle these problems. Until then, it is simply what society (the aggregation of sovereign consumers) has chosen (chapter 3).

There are, of course, overt forms of sacrifice, even in a society that talks as if sacrifice would be a new, uncalled-for burden. Police officers walk into the line of fire, firefighters enter burning buildings, and soldiers go into battle, all to protect us and ensure our way of life. Noble sacrifice, though, is only for these few, today's gladiators and knights. The rest of us not only are absolved from making such sacrifices but are expected not to make any at all, certainly not in the commercial realm, not in our producing and consuming, not in that all-important task of keeping the economic engine primed. The marketplace is about opportunity, about meeting basic needs. And if the consuming slides from basics to indulgences, from mere choice to greed, from renewing to mining, "the economy" cannot and should not distinguish. Excess is only in the eye of the moralizer; sufficiency is for traditionalists and rejectionists, for people with a "different set of values." What the sovereign consumer chooses is necessary and right; anything less is sacrifice, for the consumer, for the economy, and, therefore, for society.

In game theory terms, sacrifice is the "sucker's payoff" in the Prisoner's Dilemma. Only a fool would choose a course of action that risks maximizing one's payoff. Indeed, sacrifice is where the magic of the marketplace and social Darwinism join: pursuing one's self-interest automatically aggregates into the public interest, and if some are left behind in the process, society is still better off, because the winners increase the overall pie. Besides, the winners are the most fit and should survive; the losers bring down the average and should be weeded out— that is, sacrificed. In this utilitarian vision, the losers—the powerless, the poor, the backward—are expendable and are hence rendered invisible, their sacrifice covert and thus acceptable.

In short, to sacrifice *in* the marketplace is anathema; to sacrifice *for* the marketplace is acceptable and necessary, especially if the sacrifice is covert (i.e., if we don't talk about it or look for it) and the risks are incurred by a select few. In a society ruled by sovereign consumers, where private purchases define the very identity of those consumers, overt sacrifice is relegated to the public realm, to those relatively rare instances where heroes are made, not the everyday stuff of driving an industrial and postindustrial economy: buying is what consumers do, and the more they buy, the better.

Positive versus Negative

I have hinted at the observation that sacrifice has both positive and negative connotations. Both involve giving something up in exchange for a higher value. The difference is in the expectation of loss, given a role. Distinguishing between positive and negative sacrifice, I have found, is a handy way to frame the modern conundrum of sacrifice.

Positive sacrifice is exemplified by the parent who sacrifices time and resources to raise a child. The typical parent will hardly express her efforts as sacrifice; it is just what parents do, part of having children. It is, in short, inherent in the role. To put it more caustically, if one does not want to sacrifice for children, one should not be a parent. Similarly, an artist sacrifices income and job security to do the art. It is not a negative sacrifice, because "doing the art" is what it means to assume the role of artist. It is sacrifice, though, because one is giving up economic and social benefit for the higher value of doing the art. One willingly "makes a sacrifice."

Negative sacrifice is exemplified by the coal miners and chemical workers who sell their labor for a paycheck but actually give up their future health. It is exemplified by the volunteer soldier who sacrifices income, education, and, possibly, his life to protect the nation (positive sacrifice) and then, while serving, loses the mortgage, forcing his spouse to seek charity (negative sacrifice). Here, one is "being sacrificed."[5]

The roles of employee and soldier have no inherent "giving up" of health and economic security. These negative sacrifices are not part of the bargain; they are unexpected and perceived as undeserved. They do not fit the role.

And so it is that in the role of consumer there is no inherent "giving up" beyond trading money for goods and services. As a consumer, I *only* engage in the commercial exchange. I do not run a government, express my devotion to a deity, feed the poor, or save the environment; I just buy. And I buy the best goods and services I can for the money. Nothing more. To put it differently, anything less, any forgoing of "market value" by the consumer, is a sacrifice, a *negative sacrifice*, a stepping out of role, a denial of the inherent nature of *being a consumer*, as contradictory as being a parent yet losing no sleep, as being an artist yet punching a time clock. To be a consumer, including a green consumer like Kermit, should be easy.

This construction of the non-sacrificial nature of the role of consumer then leads to a crucial question for those of us concerned about overconsumption, an uneconomical economy, and values beyond market values: what is the appropriate role for reversing the trends in environmental degradation? Is there any role for the consumer? Logically, the answer is no: consumers do not save the environment, they just buy. To underscore this critical point, if I want to help the victims of Darfur, do I shift my consumption patterns? If so, which? How? To what expected effect? To save refugees, just as to save the environment, one does not shift consumption patterns. One shifts to a different role: *citizen*. Even if one can imagine some change in consumption that would help Darfur refugees (proceeds from a T-shirt sale go to the refugees, say), to have any effect would require widespread organizing. And that organizing is not buying; it is not what consumers do, it is what citizens do (and, in this case, what others—government officials, journalists, soldiers—do). And it's not easy.

At root, then, sacrifice (whether positive or negative) is a value-neutral notion, contingent upon role-specific expectations. I suggest the following definition:

Sacrifice is the willful, informed "giving up" of something valued for a higher value.

I value a good night's sleep, but I'll willingly give it up to care for my baby; I value my personal security but will forfeit (or risk) it to defend my country. I do this because this is what it means to be a parent or a soldier. So sacrifice is *role specific*: a sleepless night makes sense for a parent, not for a line worker (worrying about tomorrow's line speed, for instance); risking one's life makes sense for a soldier, not for a coal miner. And the value—the higher value—varies with the risk taken. The sacrifice a soldier makes in a war zone is not the same as the one a soldier makes on a relief mission, even if the goal—protecting lives—is the same.[6]

It may well be that nearly all roles entail sacrifice. Parenting, soldiering, teaching, legislating, adjudicating, running a business are, after all, "other-interested," about relations (however personal, strategic, or power-driven), about the coherence and legitimacy and meaning of the larger society and one's place in it. Interestingly, the only roles in modern life without an inherent element of sacrifice, it seems, are the commercial—consumer, producer, investor. In these roles, the ideal role is one devoid of friendship and enmity, of power and weakness, even of competition and cooperation. In these roles, it's all about the transaction—anonymous, abstract, disconnected. Price determines all, not relations, obligations, responsibilities, or justice. There's no commitment.[7] It is the ultimate juvenile playground—no responsibilities, no rules, and a never-ending flow of food and goodies; all fun, no constraint; all indulgence, no consequence; all new and improved, no tradition and no looking back.

In highly individualistic, open, market-driven, commercially oriented, and democratic societies (such as the United States), the negative side of sacrifice prevails ("People won't sacrifice; why should they?"). In other societies—in fact, in the great preponderance of societies across cultures and across time—the positive prevails. "Outside our own [Western] cultural context, sacrifice appears to be a nearly universal practice whose effects have been understood as positive," writes political theorist Karen Litfin. "While the forms that sacrifice has taken across human culture have varied greatly, anthropologists generally agree that it functions to promote social cohesion and a sense of deep relationship with cosmos and transcendental forces."[8]

What is important to recognize from the standpoint of overconsumption and the goal of treading softly and living within our means is that no society employs strictly a positive or a strictly negative notion of sacrifice; every society relies on a mix. Getting the right mix for the assigned goal is the challenge. In a frontier economy where rapid industrialization is the goal, the negative makes sense: to get people to extract, produce, consume, and dispose, and do so rapidly and thoroughly and at ever greater levels. The requisite norm is some combination of adventure, exploration, and risk taking. The associated norm of sacrifice must be negative: sacrifice is holding back, being reticent, even weak and cowardly. Of course we should push that frontier; what are you afraid of? In a nationalistic and militaristic society bent on subjugating neighboring populations, a norm of sacrifice as defending the motherland and advancing civilization makes sense, hence, positive sacrifice.

The real issue in framing a politics of sacrifice in an advanced industrial economy is the *distribution* of positive and negative sacrifice. In communal societies (and communal segments of individualistic societies—insurance cooperatives, credit unions, and cohousing and religious groups, for example), members are expected to sacrifice for their families, their communities, and their nation. When they do it well, they are admired. They move up a notch in the social order. When they do it poorly, they lose respect, are shunned, ostracized, or banished. In individualistic societies, people who sacrifice often slip back in the social hierarchy. Soldiers come home injured and find little place in a society that values mobility and youthful health. A corporate manager takes time off to care for her ailing father and thereby misses a promotion. A committed environmentalist makes do with one car and a modest house, and friends rib him for his eccentricities and naiveté.

So as much as sacrifice—that is, sacrifice presumed to be negative—may seem anathema in modern commercial societies, it has only been distributed so, or pushed "underground," says Litfin. "Far from being an invalid or nonexistent form of human activity, [positive] sacrifice in modernity is ubiquitous but largely unconscious."[9] A careful historical examination of the origins of consumerism might reveal the sources and rationales for such a redistribution. For instance, if prudence and thrift were systematically suppressed in the United States to spur domestic consumption and absorb industrial output, all to expand the economy and create a great power,[10] then it would follow that sacrifice would be limited to acts of great heroism and (probably later) of parenting (raising the next generation's workforce and consumers) and volunteering (e.g., Kiwanis, women's clubs, Peace Corps). If positive sacrifice were deliberately limited so as to create sovereign, free-spending consumers, then we would have good reason to treat as suspect statements about individual's inability to sacrifice (even in the positive sense): Americans will never get out of their cars; to stop consuming is to ruin the economy; the American way of life is not up for negotiation. These are rhetorical claims that justify the status quo—relentless expansion, voracious consuming. They say that it is normal, even patriotic, to demand more and more and at low, low prices. They say life should be easy. They put defenders of noncommercial values (e.g., ecological integrity, stable climate, social justice, care for others) on the defensive, shifting the burden of proof and the burden of creating an economic alternative to those who see the impossibility of endless material growth and the dismissal of huge externalities, environmental and human. These claims divert attention from fundamental shifts.

The Everyday

Just as efficiency seeped out of the factory and permeated nearly every facet of modern life, all to justify a mechanistic and expansionist vision of the good life, sacrifice has been squelched, relegated to the brave (overtly heroic) and the weak (covertly worthless) but not to the man and woman on the street, relegated to patriotism and economic growth but not to provisioning and building a community.

To dismiss sacrifice in the material realm of producing and consuming is to depreciate the everyday, the small and little-noticed acts that elevate daily life, that give meaning to being someone other than a valiant soldier or a titan of industry. When my local shoe store owner gives me a deep discount, the negative version of sacrifice affords only a limited, depreciative interpretation: this is an unnecessary forfeit of profit, or he is "buying" customer loyalty. Without an everyday notion of positive sacrifice, it is impossible (or very difficult for the commercially oriented) to interpret the deep discount as what he and I know it is: one of many acts (such as my volunteering to sand his store floors) that cements our friendship. When I walk to work, avoiding the convenience of my car, the negative version of sacrifice again only affords a particular depreciative interpretation: He's a do-gooder, a fool who doesn't know that the gasoline he saves is trivial. What message is he trying to send? Does he really think he'll make the rest of us feel guilty or that we will imitate him? In other words, a consumerist ideology, by disallowing a noble notion of everyday sacrifice, can ascribe only irrationality to my "consumer choice" of walking to work. It cannot accept that for me walking confers numerous personal and social benefits, not the least of which are fresh air, exercise, uninterrupted mental space (a scarce item even riding the bus, let alone driving), chance encounters with friends and strangers (including the town's homeless "regulars"), a sense of my community that no amount of driving or reading or discussing can match, and, yes, a decreased impact on others and the environment.[11]

So the depreciation of sacrifice in the everyday, the denial of a positive sacrifice for all but the few, is the denial of other-interestedness, of the chance to pursue higher purposes—democratic participation (aside from mere voting), performing good work, and living within our ecological means, for instance. It is to relegate people to mere consumers and mere workers. It is to hand over the big challenges to the experts, the global managers, to those with the data and the funds. It is to deny citizenship. It is to dismiss as foolish the act of an old man planting an oak sapling (knowing he will never see its majestic state), a toddler helping an adult pick up a piece of chalk, a teenager committed to saving the planet.

Righting the Consumer Economy

A consumer economy all too readily becomes a consumer society, giving the appearance of full democratic participation. We are all consumers, after all; we all make choices in the marketplace, voluntarily. But it is a society supremely organized to absolve individuals—consumers, producers, investors, and even rule makers—of responsibility. Consequently, the consumer society can, and does, displace costs in time and place. It concentrates benefits among the powerful few and distributes the costs to the many, often disproportionately to the disempowered. It severs feedback loops that would otherwise put a brake on endless expansion. It constructs a notion of the good life that centers on goods, not on relations, not on service, not on citizenship. And it all seems so rational, so historically inevitable. But it is not the basis of an ecological order; there is no ethic of living within our means.

The answer to overconsumption is not better consuming by better-informed consumers. The sovereign consumer must be dethroned; sacrifice must be elevated, restored to its proper, "make sacred" pedestal. No, sacrifice is not easy, but few worthwhile things are. What to do?

For a start, be a citizen, a neighbor, a parent, a friend, a guardian, a steward before being a consumer. And celebrate the positive sacrifice in that good work. Then set about building a positive economy, at whatever scale is manageable. And be economical about it. The hedonistic, growth-manic, cost-displacing industrial order, the order that more and more feels like a house of cards, must give way to an ecological order with a home economy, one grounded in place and with a view to the distant past and the far future.

Work, Workers, and Working: Toward an Economy That Works

Remember that shoe store owner in chapter 8, Beppo Road-sweeper in chapter 7, the chainsaw operator, landscaper, and master woodworker (okay, wannabe master woodworker) in chapter 6, and the lobster catcher in chapter 5? These people (or characters), you probably noticed, have something in common. Their personalities and ideologies and socioeconomic position may vary greatly. But they all perform particular kinds of work, ones quite at odds with the conventional notion of "work" in the current industrial, consumerist, and expansionist order. Here I wish to construct an image of work that builds in limits at the same time that it promotes a sense of meaning and counters the demeaning notion of work. For concrete examples we already have these characters; a few more are to come. But I invite the reader to do me one better: First, ask yourself what instance of work, paid or unpaid, was especially gratifying in your life, what work was challenging, rewarding, engaging. Next, ask a friend (or an enemy, or someone who you find quite boring) the same thing. My guess is that if you get positive answers (and I always do when I ask this question), you will see yourself or that person in the following discussion. If so, and if you like what you read, imagine a business or a community organization or a government agency or an entire economy that encourages just this kind of work, work that is at once satisfying and self-limiting. If you go that far, and add the frames of positive sacrifice and citizen first, you are a long ways toward imagining a home economy in an ecological order. Then think of these frames as tools for actually enacting that order.

To start with, let's take "work" to be those activities that, necessary or not, burdensome or not, satisfy the actor in some important way. They demand focused attention and acquired skills and result in a sense of competence, of "doing a job right." Examples include creating a business, expressing oneself artistically, and rearing a child. Now a bit of history, long forgotten in industrial society's rush to push product and consume consumables. This account connects to chapter 7 drawing again on the work of historian and social critic Christopher Lasch.[1] It aims to further develop the idea (and the ideal) of an "economical economy."[2]

The Producerist

We start in the late nineteenth-century United States, where the ideals of progress and populism coexisted and, in many ways, competed. Three strands of thought and practice can be discerned in the emergence of the progressive ideal and the corresponding submergence of the populist ideal. I call their proponents the rejectionists, the expansionists, and the producerists.[3]

The *rejectionists*, possibly typified by the Luddites then and the Amish now, opposed much of the advances of science and technology. They valued self-reliance and community cohesion. They could adopt new technologies, but only selectively, only when the technologies did not disrupt existing social relations. The *expansionists* were just the opposite. Engineers and economists embraced scientific and technological advance. Boosters promoted cities and railroads and telegraphs and just about any "new way of doing things," anything "modern." Public officials and the media extolled the virtues of ever-increasing variety and quantity of goods. If innovation and, especially, efficiency seeking in the form of a division of labor, mechanization, labor mobility, and economies of scale came at the cost of worker dependence and alienation and increasing concentration of economic power, then the expansionists knew that the long-term benefits to individuals and to the nation (as a great power) far exceeded those costs. Continuous expansion was the essence of progress.[4]

The third group, the *producerists*, have largely faded from historical memory, eclipsed by expansionism. The producerists were a mostly unorganized collection of artisans, master craftspeople, small shop owners, and independent, yeoman farmers. Many were tinkers, inventors of the very technologies that excited the expansionists and helped propel the nation to greatness. The producerists were businesspeople, committed to making products, selling them, and earning a profit. They were also committed—some might say, fiercely committed—to the notion that political independence was inextricably intertwined with economic independence. Democracy depended on a populace that could produce for itself, not just in the aggregate, not just at the national level, but at the level of the individual, the household, and the immediate community. "Freedom could not flourish in a nation of hirelings," wrote Lasch.[5] These small proprietors in the United States, England, and France resisted the expansionists' label for them, "working class"; instead they saw themselves as *producers*, people who identified their enemy not as employers (they were self-employed, after all) but as parasitic bankers, speculators, monopolists, and middlemen. Despite the ascendance of the expansionists through the nineteenth century, the producerist movement, if it can be called a movement, persisted until the turn of the century. "Even in the factory," Lasch writes, "artisans often retained control of the rhythm and design of production; and it was their resistance to employers' attempts to introduce a more complicated division of labor and to replace skilled craftsmen with operatives, as much as the fight for higher wages and shorter hours, that shaped working-class radicalism right down to the end of the nineteenth century."[6] It was precisely at this time in the United States—the early twentieth century—that expansionism achieved its ultimate conversion of everyday life: from producerism (the population was still overwhelmingly rural) to consumerism.

But producerism survived through the nineteenth century in part because the populace as a whole still believed that there was virtue in work, that making goods and services that were useful to others was a higher pursuit than merely accumulating wealth. Their vision of a proper industrial order (the producerists did not reject science and technology, let alone profit making) might be best captured by the notion of "a calling," a term quite common not so long ago but largely supplanted today with terms like "job" and "employment." A calling not only guided people's choice of productive enterprise but embodied a sense of intermittency and sufficiency (chapter 5). Traditionally, a calling had three elements, each of which suggests a source of limits in the nature of self-directed, producerist work.[7]

The first is *fit*. In a calling, individuals seek work that fits their skills and aptitudes. Some are meant to be poets, others road sweepers. This is absolutely contrary to the prevailing modern view that one "gets a job" to make as much money as possible and that the best jobs are those that pay the most. Pursuing jobs to maximize an income stream and consume freely has no limits. A calling, by contrast, is limited by the fit. From a progressive, liberal perspective, this would be, of course, a constraint on freedom. But freedom to do what? Earn and spend as much as possible. The liberal perspective accepts the nostrums of the turn-of-the-century boosters by assigning personal value and self-worth to consumption, not production, not to the deliberately and freely chosen pursuit (at least in the ideal) of one's calling.

The second element in a calling is *service* to one's community through production. Producers make items they deem useful to others. Notably, this judgment is made by the *producer*, not, as in the belief system of the contemporary consumer economy, by the sovereign consumer (chapter 3). In a calling, producers do not merely respond to demand. Automakers could not throw up their hands and exclaim, "But the consumers *demand* the gas guzzlers; we just produce them." Caveat emptor, "Let the buyer beware," has no meaning in the context of a calling where the producer is responsible for the quality of the item, where the producer is accountable. In a calling, consumers are not sovereign; producers are. Yet they work *in service to others*. As a result, pride of workmanship prevails over the techniques of salesmanship. Quality is preferred to quantity. This emphasis on service and quality and, in many contexts, direct, face-to-face contact imposes on the producer limits that are largely unimaginable in today's large-scale, specialized, limited-liability corporate world. And these limits are not imposed externally, by law or religion, nor chosen by a company so as to be the "good corporate citizen." Rather, they arise as a rational means of operating over time *in a community*, of ensuring, as the producerists always advocated, a livelihood for themselves, their community, and their successors.

The third element is, traditionally, service to God. A secular version might be service to the *long-term welfare* of present and future generations. Here, too, service is not to the whims and gullibilities of consumers but to the producers' sense and the community's sense of what is right, what is truly good, not to what sells as a good.

The producerist ideal thus embodies a profound sense of meaning in work. It rejects the producer-consumer, work-leisure dichotomies of the consumer economy and the "discipline" of the clock and the supervisor. Instead, it promotes the discipline of good work. "That way you enjoy your work," recall Beppo Roadsweeper saying, "which is important, because then you make a good job of it. And that's how it ought to be."[8] The producerist ideal promotes the values of identity, economic independence, and citizenship through self-directed proprietorship. Inherent in such a vision is *self*-discipline, striving for purpose. Lasch puts it this way:

> Luxury for all: such was the noble dream of progress. Populists [producerists], on the other hand, regarded a competence, as they would have called it—a piece of earth, a small shop, a useful calling—as a more reasonable as well as a more worthy ambition. "Competence" had rich moral overtones; it referred to the livelihood conferred by property but also to the skills required to maintain it. The ideal of universal proprietorship embodied a humbler set of expectations than the ideal of universal consumption, universal access to a proliferating supply of goods. At the same time, it embodied a more strenuous and morally demanding definition of the good life. The progressive conception of history implied a society of supremely cultivated consumers; the populist [producerist] conception, a whole world of heroes.[9]

In terms of an ecological order, the producerist ideal means that one accepts the demands of others and nature, not resisting but welcoming limits to ever-increasing material throughput. In short, it is *living well by living well within our means.*

Globalizers may see a world of consumers, but those who understand "real work," who see intimate connections between work and citizenship and sustainability, see a world of citizens, citizens grounded in place, who work and thrive and contribute. These "heroes" are ennobled, not threatened, by limits. A century ago Simon Patten, economist and founding father of consumer theory, concluded that "all traditional restraints on consumption" should be "eliminated," and over the following decades, all restraints were indeed eliminated. Now, given the fundamental shifts under way, it is time to construct new "restraints," traditional or nontraditional. It is time for a wholly new emphasis, one that connects the limits of the planet to the limits of everyday practice. It is time for an ethic that celebrates not consumers as purchasers but workers as citizens, not unending expansion but working and living within immutable constraints. Consumption no longer unifies a nation and elevates the individual, as Patten and his successors have seen it. Rather, as practiced, consumption undermines the biophysical foundations on which nations and individuals rest.

The producerist ideal failed in the nineteenth century for many reasons, not the least of which was, as noted, the lure of expansionism. But it also might have failed because it lacked *central organizing principles*. It was probably not enough for producers to argue that they wanted to keep their small shops and independent farms when progress increasingly meant bigger factories, bigger supply chains, and finally, with the turn-of-the-century development of consumer theory in economics, marketing in business schools, and demand stimulation in government, all of which resulted in bigger consumer markets. "I'm figgering on biggering," the Onceler exclaims in Dr. Seuss's children's classic *The Lorax*. "And BIGGERING and BIGGERING and BIGGERING, turning MORE Truffula Trees into Thneeds which everyone, EVERYONE, *EVERYONE* needs!"[10] Expansion was the order of the day, the "natural order of things," the imperative of an efficiency-obsessed era, the raison d'être of a consumer economy.

Today, with the imperative to construct an ecological order, we must translate the self-evident limits of a single planet into the limits of everyday life. For that, organizing principles might include intermittency, sufficiency, capping, and sourcing (chapter 5). Such a translation is unlikely, arguably impossible, under the logic of an expansionist, industrial, and consumer economy, where specialization, large-scale operation, and consumer demand prevail. It is possible, though, when work is more a calling than a job and, we will next see, when work follows the rhythms of task and nature, when work is self-directed and generalist—in short, when work is less alienating and more connecting.

Work That Connects

Work promotes connection when, at its most basic level, it occurs at the interface of ecological functioning and human functioning. The fishing and hunting, planting and irrigating, logging and drilling is where resource use is decided and where feedback from the biophysical system is registered. Activity in the realms of policy and markets—legislating, adjudicating, administering, investing, producing, consuming—may function similarly. But decision making in these realms, especially in advanced industrial economies, is physically separated from primary resource extraction and resource use questions.

Work also promotes connection when the *rhythm* of work derives from a *time sense* that is "natural." A modern industrial economy structures time as mechanical time. It embodies a vision of the good life that cannot allow idleness or caring for others or preparing food or serving on committees or any number of other tasks in the household or community economies. Rather, the divisibility of tasks and the expansion of consumer goods provides the measure of time, a measure that is inherently short term from an ecological point of view, that always leans toward this year's output, even this quarter's earnings, more than to this generation's needs, let alone to that of the

next and the next. With different conceptions of time, though—
what I term "natural" time and task-based time—a different vision can arise, one more attuned to human need for association,
meaning, and challenge as well as to ecosystem functioning.
It is from such conceptions that work and, hence, consumption and everyday connection to the material and social worlds
arise. And it is in these expanded notions of time (beyond the
mechanical) and work (beyond mere employment) that identity and satisfaction coincide with restrained consumption. It is
here that time and work serve as essential building blocks for
connection in the home economy of an ecological order.

The first feature of a natural rhythm of work is *idiosyncratic
regularity* (what the early industrialists derided as "irregular-
ity"). Given a variety of work and productive opportunities,
some of which are necessary to survival, some of which promote well-being, individuals tend to parcel their work time—
their day, their week, their seasons—into regularized episodes
of intense work followed by rest or social interaction. One may
begin the morning with physical activity (e.g., surveying, harvesting, building), stop to eat, resume the physical activity, then
shift to mental pursuits (e.g., calculating, corresponding, plan-
ning), then to artistic endeavors (e.g., writing, gardening, painting, playing music). All of this may be interspersed with care of
children and the elderly.

The regularity of this pattern should not be confused with the
regularity imposed by mechanized routines such as that found
on the assembly line. There, the clock and the organization of
wage labor compel standardized behavior among all workers.
Some are hired only for physical work, others for mental work,
and the choice and distribution of work is externally imposed.
Here, it is chosen—chosen by the "worker." The regularity derives from the need in one's productive pursuits for familiarity
and predictability, on the one hand, and variety and challenge,

on the other. Each individual's rhythm is particular, though. Some are inclined to lengthy periods of monotonous, familiar routines, others to continual exploration and experimentation. Given the choice, individuals will develop and maintain their own rhythms of work, their own combination of toil, expression, and nurturing. And they will be driven to do so because it is in such work that individuals achieve a sense of competency and self-worth. These people are not the individuals a consumer economy constructs, though. In a consumer society individuals just buy.

The second feature of a rhythm of work is *built-in limits*. Physical capacities are the most obvious source of limits. Exhaustion and occupational maladies such as carpal tunnel syndrome are extreme forms. Given a choice, individuals will readily shift from physically demanding work to rest or other forms of work long before debilitating fatigue sets in. Psychological limits may be less obvious but no less significant. Humans have a reservoir of directed attention that can be allocated to tasks but cannot be drawn down indefinitely without restoration. I can write for several hours, teach for a couple more, and attend a meeting or two. But if I don't then go for a walk, rearrange my files, swing a hammer, or pull some weeds, I'm worn out. I'm irritable and intolerant. Colleagues and family members can provide empirical substantiation. One colleague, a psychologist, Raymond De Young, tells me that research indeed shows that effective restorative activities include walks, cleaning, and hobbies, as well as playing games, sports, and music. These are restorative to the extent they

1. temporarily take the actor (physically or mentally) out of his or her overly demanding environment;

2. provide a new environment (physical or mental) in which one can "lose oneself" and explore;

3. offer the actor a degree of fascination (some challenge or stimulation but not so much as to further drain directed attention).

Sleep, even a full night's sleep, cannot by itself restore directed attention, especially in the face of a large sleep deficit.[11]

Regularly shifting from a demanding activity to a monotonous activity can be restorative and can thus enhance both activities, heightening an individual's life satisfaction and meaning. Notably, that satisfaction and meaning do not come only from the "higher" forms of work, the mental or artistic, say, but from the menial, too. Getting all my leaves raked before the first big storm is still a job well done. Most important, the two kinds of activity are *self-limiting*, physically and psychologically. Alternating between the two compels a self-directed individual to limit physically and mentally draining activities. This mode of work intersects with ecosystem functioning via time reckoning.

Time reckoning is the process by which we sense the passage of time. In preindustrial societies, time reckoning was predominantly *nature-driven* and *task-based*. The "time" to plant and to harvest and the "time" to have a child were dictated by season and physical maturity and culturally evolved proscriptions. There was a time to work, a time to play, someone once wrote and others sang. And the time it takes to create, to invent, to explore, or to experiment was determined by the task, not by a taskmaster with a clock. Anyone who has created a recipe, designed a landscape, or written a book knows how hard it is to answer the question "How long did it take?" One may look for a clock-based answer because mechanistic time reckoning is dominant in contemporary society, but it makes little sense. Ask a parent how long it took to teach the child to be responsible. Ask professionals how long it takes to design a product, compose a song, build a winning coalition. Hours and days just do not capture the *quality* of the passage of time in such endeavors. One just does them. Their time is up when they are done. Or, as Gandalf tells Frodo in the movie version of *The Lord of the Rings: The Fellowship of the Ring*, "A wizard is never late. . . . Nor is he early. He arrives precisely when he means to."[12]

Although clock-based time reckoning dominates contemporary thought and practice, it has by no means extinguished the preindustrial forms. Task-based time exists, as noted, in the home, but also on the playground, along the trout stream, and in the meeting house. What is common to all is *self-direction*.

Social psychologist Melvin Kohn surveyed a wide-ranging set of studies on work, including longitudinal psychological studies in the United States and other industrialized countries, and found that a research consensus exists on the conditions that promote well-being through work:

> Of all the structural imperatives of the job, those that determine how much opportunity, even necessity, the worker has for exercising occupational *self-direction* [the use of initiative, thought, and independent judgment] are the most important for personality. . . .
>
> Exercising self-direction in work—doing work that is substantively complex, not being closely supervised, not working at routinized tasks—is conducive to favorable evaluations of self, an open and flexible orientation to others, and effective intellectual functioning.

In short, "people *thrive* in meeting occupational challenges,"[13] in pursuing purposeful work, not in purchasing that which is "provided by a salesman."[14] They can certainly derive meaning from consumption; they can, for instance, approach shopping as a challenge, as a modern form of hunting and gathering. But it is reasonable to assume that the meaning derived from shopping, following fashion, and pursuing the latest and biggest car is nowhere near the same as the "thriving" provided by purposeful work. Ephemeral pleasures do not accumulate into sustained gratification and meaning the way persistent, disciplined work does. Furthermore, the purposes of "good work" are self-chosen, whereas the purposes of consuming are largely determined by others—commercial boosters in industry and government, even educators and environmentalists. Self-direction, once again, is found in work, not in buying.

Possibly the best evidence for the "thriving" of self-directed work and its associated natural rhythm, though, is negative: a massive social engineering effort was undertaken to overcome popular resistance to industrialization. Why would such a wrenching effort be needed if the industrial order made sense? The answer appears to be that it made sense to the few, not the many. In nonindustrial, unsupervised settings, it appears that humans do indeed perform just enough work to meet their needs (as opposed to the needs of absentee owners and distant landlords), and they perform just enough wage work to meet *some* of their needs, leaving adequate time to meet other needs in other ways.

Although it is easy to dismiss such work patterns as anomalous or primitive, it is at least equally logical to see them as suggestive of a perfectly "natural" tendency in work, namely, as an innate ability to recognize when enough is enough. The general case in which it occurs may not be when modernity meets traditionalism but whenever humans have considerable discretion over when, how much, and how they work. Preindustrial peoples are an obvious case. But the evidence suggests that so is self-employment, or any productive activity with a degree of autonomy, a degree of independence from outside forces, especially the coercive and manipulative.

In situations where individuals have a high level of autonomous choice, then, and not just consumer choice, but producer, or *productive choice*, limiting one's work and hence productive output is perfectly rational. "Natural work" employs natural and task-based forms of time reckoning that, unlike the mechanistic, which can be repeatedly divided and accelerated, are governed by forces that cannot be manipulated—by physiology (sleep and waking, highs and lows through the day), cognition (an individual's capacity for interpersonal relations is limited to some 150 individuals), diurnal and seasonal cycles, and social interaction (cooperation and competition, consensus making and strategic gaming). These are all forces that establish immutable limits. No amount of tinkering can change this.

If self-limitation in self-managed work is "natural," as much a part of human nature as choosing a mate and organizing for self-defense, then it follows that so is self-restraint in consumption and, hence, in resource use. Humans do not always want more. Goods may be good but more goods may not be better. Humans make trade-offs not just in their purchasing and investing but, given the opportunity, in their working, their producing, their productive being. Humans do not choose to consume more and more if the trade-off is between, on the one hand, unpleasant, meaningless, unrewarding yet monetarily compensated "work" and, on the other, pleasant, meaningful, and rewarding "work," whether or not compensated for monetarily. Simply put, if individuals have choices not just in what they buy or where they invest, but in the quantity and quality of work they perform, they are likely to minimize externally directed, routinized activities, those activities dependent on monetary compensation or, in the extreme, on coercion for their performance—for example, wage labor, contract hire, paid employment. At the same time, they are likely to maximize internally satisfying work—self-employment, independent business, family farming, freelancing, consulting. One result is restraint in income-generating production and, hence, in the purchasing of goods, that is, in consumption. Restraint is not self-abnegation, any more than limits are confinement. It is choosing less material use than what is possible in exchange for nonmaterial benefits: less material in the short term for more (or more secure) material in the long term. Here it is exchanging less income and, hence, less purchasable goods, for more gratifying work, not just having a job and collecting a paycheck.

The archetype for the propensity to restrain work and consumption may be the artist who works the day job only enough to make ends meet and then practices, performs, writes, and teaches the rest of the time because such art-related activities are the most rewarding. Close to artists might be independent scholars. In the business world, there are independent farmers, fishers, and loggers who often say that it is their love of the land or the sea and the associated way of life that keeps them from taking a more lucrative, wage-earning job. Entrepreneurs, store owner-operators, and publishers may also fit the mold. For them, a major motivation is to have one's own business, to be self-employed, to contribute directly to one's community. The desire to have one's own business may be as close to a universal yearning as any economic goal even in, or especially in, contemporary industrial societies.

In all these activities, from art to farming to self-employed business endeavors, individuals make money. And they undoubtedly prefer to make more money. But these occupations suggest that in the trade-off between burdensome work ("just a job") and rewarding productive activity ("making something happen"), many people do choose productive activity, however poorly compensated monetarily. Many people do forgo the income of "gainful employment" and the consumption opportunities that go with it. Many people live well by living within their means.

An economy grounded in place, in one's social community and ecological community, is a practical economy. And the essential practice of a practical economy is work—work that is productive, engaging, and self-directed. It is work that respects others, other people and other systems, including ecosystems. Such work is satisfying, useful, and self-limiting. It is economical. What is more, it is imaginable, not because the contemporary economy encourages it—far from it—but because so many people enact it, however anomalous their acts may be, however much their practice challenges the consumerist and expansionist order.

10

Speaking of the Environment: Two Worlds, Two Languages

In a land not so far away, Sufficiencius grew up in a small but thriving town. From a young age, he would ride his bicycle up the hill to Utilitarius's house, a spacious but unpretentious home with a magnificent view. Utilitarius, a pillar of the community, a successful man on many dimensions, would provide cookies and milk, and the two would talk.

Now a young man, Sufficiencius preferred cappuccino and "everything" bagels, which Utilitarius tried to provide. Often as not, though, he just put out cookies and milk. And the conversations were more broad-ranging, even philosophical. Sometimes they were strained. As much as Sufficiencius respected Utilitarius's views and his life accomplishments, Utilitarius's world seemed so different from Sufficiencius's. In fact, Sufficiencius had become increasingly exasperated by Utilitarius's positions.

It wasn't the difference in age, Sufficiencius thought, so much as the difference in worldviews, in the very language the two used. Their analogies and images and expectations were so different, so . . . worlds apart.

Today Sufficiencius was determined to get to the heart of the matter, at least with respect to one of his passions—the environment. He told Utilitarius how concerned he was about environmental degradation, how he just couldn't understand how, with all that is known about environmental trends, people could just continue with business as usual, as if there's no tomorrow, as if we have a couple more planets to burn.

The two sat down on separate couches, as usual, cookies and milk on the coffee table, with an array of picture windows offering a spectacular view of the town below.

Utilitarius: Listen. I like the environment as much as anyone. But we have to keep the economy going, produce the goods that people need. And maintain law and order, defend our borders. These things come first.

Sufficiencius: Yes, those things are important, but—

Utilitarius: Important? They are essential.

Sufficiencius: But so is the environment.

Utilitarius: For you and your nature-loving friends, maybe. But for the rest of us, those who work hard to generate real wealth, the wealth that gives us the ability to protect ourselves—and the environment—it's the economy, and national security. They come first.

Sufficiencius: All right, we're not going to agree on that, but please tell me what you mean by "the environment."

Utilitarius: Sure. The environment is where nature is. For example, I go fly fishing in the mountains every summer. It's beautiful. There's talk about damming that river, but I'm against it. A lot of people enjoy it, and not just us fly fishers but hikers and boaters and birdwatchers too—you know, your type.

Sufficiencius: I imagine quite a few bears and birds and a lot of other creatures enjoy that river, too, not to mention the farmers and ranchers who irrigate with it, and the townspeople who draw their drinking water from it.

Utilitarius: I suppose so.

Sufficiencius: Okay, so when you talk about "the environment" you mean green places—parks and mountains and rivers and whatnot.

Utilitarius: Yeah, places to get away from it all, to relax, have fun. Studies show, you know, that green places are good for you; they help restore your mental energies.

Sufficiencius: So I've heard. But I'm still not clear what you mean by "the environment" when you talk about the economy and producing goods and generating wealth.

Utilitarius: Oh, that. Well, in that case the environment is where we get the raw materials. You see, it's only when we make things from nature that they have value. The economy, you know, is all about creating value.

Sufficiencius: What about the value that's already there, in the rivers and fish and trees and soil?

Utilitarius: Oh, I see. We need to go back to basics, Econ 101. Now, the first thing is—

Sufficiencius: Actually, I've studied economics. I think I understand it pretty well. What I don't understand is how people like you think about "the environment."

Utilitarius: All right. Let's start with a tree. It's just standing there, doing no one any good. When someone cuts it and makes it into lumber and then a house, then it does some good. Then it has value.

Sufficiencius: And the tree is part of "the environment"?

Utilitarius: Yes, along with iron ore and oil and farmland and all that.

Sufficiencius: It's a warehouse.

Utilitarius: You might say that. Actually, it's more like a store.

Sufficiencius: How so?

Utilitarius: A store is stocked with useful items. If I need something I go there, check the price, and buy it.

Sufficiencius: When you need something you buy it, right? Fork over your hard-earned money.

Utilitarius: Right. Nothing's free. Everything has a cost.

Sufficiencius: But a forest isn't like a store. When it's clear-cut, it doesn't just come back the way it was.

Utilitarius: Sure it does. You replant, just like a storeowner restocks.

Sufficiencius: And there's always more to stock the shelves with? Never a shortage.

Utilitarius: That's right, or just about. Listen. If a bunch of us go to the store for, say, lumber, our demand not only takes boards off the shelves, it also drives the price up. The two, declining inventory and rising price, signal to the wood products manufacturer to supply more lumber.

Sufficiencius: And the timber companies always have more timber to cut?

Utilitarius: That's right. They grow trees on their land just like a farmer grows corn. Or they use public lands reserved precisely for timber harvesting. Or they go to other countries. There's plenty of timber—you can be sure of that.

Sufficiencius: What I'm sure of is that deforestation is happening all over the world.

Utilitarius: Look. When this country was young, we cut our forests. It's part of what it takes to build a great nation. Who are you to tell others they can't do the same? Besides, when they put their timber on the market, they get a good price. It's not like we're stealing it or anything.

Sufficiencius: The wonders of the market. Prices settle all.

Utilitarius: Now you're getting the picture.

Sufficiencius: That was sarcasm, actually.

Utilitarius: I knew that. But it missed the mark. Markets do work wonders.

Sufficiencius: Like beautiful machines.

Utilitarius: In fact, they are. Like nature: one big, wonderful machine.

Sufficiencius: Huh?

Utilitarius: You're the nature lover. You oughta know that.

Sufficiencius: Do explain.

Utilitarius: Nature is a system of interlocking pieces. Minerals, air, water, rivers, lakes. They all fit together, just like the pistons and cylinders, nuts and bolts of an internal combustion engine.

Sufficiencius: And organisms?

Utilitarius: Yeah, those too. They all fit together. When they fit well, all in balance, things work. When they don't, they need fixing, some fine-tuning or new parts or a complete overhaul.

Sufficiencius: And sometimes you just junk the whole thing and start over.

Utilitarius: Right, you're getting it.

Sufficiencius: Let's see if I do "get it." If humans tamper too much with natural systems—this "machine"—they should back off?

Utilitarius: No! They should fix it.

Sufficiencius: What? Fix what?

Utilitarius: They should fix whatever's not working right. If a river floods, you build levees. You wouldn't step back and let it destroy people's homes, would you? If cropland isn't getting high yields, you add fertilizer. You wouldn't let people starve, would you?

Sufficiencius: Now I think I get it. So when the climate goes haywire, you put iron filings in the oceans and mirrors in space?

Utilitarius: Now you got it!

Sufficiencius: I was being sarcastic again.

Utilitarius: I don't know much about filings and mirrors, but if this climate change thing is real we need to fix it, that's for sure.

Sufficiencius: Okay, let me see if I got this.

Utilitarius: Without the sarcasm?

Sufficiencius: I'll try. Humans mess up the climate system, so the answer is to mess with it some more?

Utilitarius: I can see you're having trouble with some fundamental concepts, like supply and demand and technological innovation. So let's try another angle.

Sufficiencius: Hold on. Before you do, let's go back to what you said about stealing timber from other countries.

Utilitarius: I said we're *not* stealing it.

Sufficiencius: I understand. But given how desperately poor people are in the global South, or corrupt, or both, the fact is they have no choice. Like they're a colony, destroying their natural resources to supply the rich North, who, by the way, sets the prices, not "the market."

Utilitarius: Whoa! Where'd you get all that? Nobody's forcing them to cut their forests.

Sufficiencius: Like I said, they have little real choice. Cut or starve: not a choice you or I would like! So what I'm hearing from you is that "the environment" is a colony too, a place where resources are abundant and cheap and other people sacrifice to provide them to us, whether under duress or with little choice in the matter.

Utilitarius: You are so pessimistic! If people have goods to sell and other people want to buy them, what's the problem? It really is a store, the more I think about it: one big exchange floor where people freely choose to buy and sell, where everyone comes out better. It amazes me you can't see that, or prefer to distort it and make it out to be a bad thing. Just amazing.

Utilitarius and Sufficiencius sat for a moment, each staring out a different window. They weren't really angry at each other; they just couldn't fathom each other's view. Finally, Sufficiencius turned to Utilitarius.

Sufficiencius: As I said, all I want to do is understand how you see "the environment." So far, it seems like the environment is completely separate from the economy.

Utilitarius: Well, the environment certainly isn't the economy. Let me try a different tack. Earlier you mentioned science. Scientists work in labs, right?

Sufficiencius: Right.

Utilitarius: Well, the environment is like one big laboratory. There are Bunsen burners, exhaust hoods, tanks full of chemicals, cages full of lab rats, and whatnot. Scientists are running experiments. Some are figuring out the origins of the universe and that kind of thing. But others, the useful ones, are inventing things, useful things.

Sufficiencius: Things that will eventually find their way to your store?

Utilitarius: That's right!

Sufficiencius: Hold on. You say the earth is a laboratory that we study and that we use to invent things. And those "things" would include houses and roads and fertilizers and heating oil and cooking oil?

Utilitarius: Yes, that's right. All the goods we need and the technologies we need to make them.

Sufficiencius: And the stock chemicals and the gas for the Bunsen burners are always available?

Utilitarius: Yes, just like in the store.

Sufficiencius: And every experiment is contained within the lab. The doors are sealed, the air filtered, the fumes exhausted.

Utilitarius: Right.

Sufficiencius: Okay, so where does the exhaust go? And the stuff collected by the filters?

Utilitarius: That's a political matter. Governments make those choices. In some places, they incinerate the waste. Others landfill it or send it to a special repository.

Sufficiencius: And for this lab to keep running there's always a place to send the waste?

Utilitarius: All right, all right. I see where you're going. Look. There are plenty of places to put this stuff—deserts, ocean bottom, upper atmosphere. You seem to be implying that there shouldn't be any waste.

Sufficiencius: That actually would be a good first step to living ecologically, since no ecosystem has waste.

Utilitarius: That's ridiculous. On my fishing trip I saw plenty of waste, from bears and birds and, yes, people. Can't get any more natural than that.

Sufficiencius: Those wastes are biological; they're broken down by microorganisms and assimilated in a short time. They become nutrients for other organisms. The wastes from your lab are radioactive or toxic or disrupt the climate.

Utilitarius: My gosh! You are so pessimistic! Do you enjoy looking at the dark side of everything?

Sufficiencius: I prefer to see all sides clearly, even the dark sides. But apparently you don't want to see the dark side of your beloved store and laboratory.

Utilitarius: Now hold on there. To you, everything is half empty.

Sufficiencius: Actually, what I see is what scientists and so many others see—namely, a planet that is half denuded, half full of wastes, half impregnated with toxic substances. And the trends don't stop.

Utilitarius: I'm just telling you how things are. You asked.

Sufficiencius: Actually, I didn't ask you to tell me how things are. I asked you to tell me how you see the world, especially "the environment," the planet's natural resources and waste sinks.

Utilitarius: What's the difference?

Sufficiencius: It's possible you're wrong, you know. It's possible your view is destroying the planet.

Utilitarius: What? *I'm* destroying the planet? After all I've done over a lifetime of hard work, creating wealth, providing jobs, and helping build a great nation so that everyone, including nature lovers and pessimists like you, can live well? *I'm* destroying the planet? You've got to be kidding!

Sufficiencius: Not you personally. Just your view, which so many in positions of influence seem to share.

Utilitarius: Well, this is getting personal now.

Sufficiencius: Okay, you're right. My mistake. Please continue.

Utilitarius took a deep breath. Sufficiencius sat back. Each stared out a different window. Clearly the discussion was veering off topic. Or was it? Neither could say for sure. Utilitarius continued.

Utilitarius: All right. Whether in the laboratory or in the factory, goods, things we need, are invented and produced. And like in all production—for that matter, all of life—there are costs and risks and by-products. We just have to carefully manage the risks and dispose of the wastes. That is something people in the laboratory can work on. Nothing's impossible.

Sufficiencius: Nothing's impossible. New technologies will solve every problem. Is that it?

Utilitarius: Yes, with the help of the market.

Sufficiencius: Oh, yeah, I almost forgot the market. But what you seem to miss again and again is the "bads." All you talk about are the so-called goods, which we presumably "need"—like electric toothbrushes and a third car, right?

Utilitarius: Those are personal choices.

Sufficiencius: But it's that lab that makes them, and marketeers who convince people to buy them. And—

Utilitarius: Hold on. There you go again, getting off track, bringing in marketing (which, by the way, provides necessary information to consumers) when what we're talking about here is the laboratory.

Sufficiencius: Okay, fair enough. So how's this: you're assuming that those experiments with all their products and by-products are all safely contained within the laboratory walls, that nothing will get away, nothing will spread on its own.

Utilitarius: Like I said, we have to be careful and manage the risks.

Sufficiencius: But how can you be careful when the entire earth is the laboratory? What happens when the experiment blows up, or it pollutes beyond the lab's boundaries, or it heats up the room beyond what's bearable?

Utilitarius: Life is full of risks. Would you prefer we just stand still, not progress, turn off the lights and crawl back in the cave? Huh?

Sufficiencius: Now *you're* getting off track. You keep talking about nature as if it's that thing "out there," something nice to visit or to extract resources from or to manipulate for human use. But I don't get the sense that, for you, nature is a system—say, a life-support system, like the life-support system of a spaceship, something that has to be carefully managed, that is fragile and cannot be abused. You see nature as something we take from but never have to *give back to*. I get the idea you don't think we can ever run out of resources.

Utilitarius: Hmmm. That is a curious view, all right. Romantic and, once again, pessimistic. But I'm a realist, and an optimist. Look. We're not running out. Throughout history there have been pessimists like you, Chicken Littles predicting doom. But the fact is, we always find more—more wood and more coal and more oil and more water. Just the other day, geologists discovered a huge underground lake in the Sahara Desert. Imagine!

Sufficiencius: It's a fossil lake. It's from ancient times. When they pump that dry, like people are doing all over the world, it won't come back.

Utilitarius: By then geologists will have discovered more. And besides, 70 percent of the earth is covered by water. We're not going to run out!

Sufficiencius: How I wish it were so.

Utilitarius: You don't have to wish it. Just stop being so damn pessimistic and get busy. Have you ever thought about becoming a geologist?

Sufficiencius: No, I have my hands full dealing with the world's depredations and your way of thinking.

Utilitarius: Oh, optimists get you down, huh?

Sufficiencius: No, cornucopians do, wishful thinkers, the market faithful, geoengineers, people who have all the answers while the planet is going to hell. Your kind are destroying everything!

Utilitarius: Whoa there! Ease up. Life's not that bad. In fact, you don't exactly look like you're starving. And correct me if I'm wrong, but isn't it "my kind" who have produced the goods that have kept you well fed and, for all I can tell, rather comfortable? You've been coming here since you could first ride a bike on your own. I applaud that. But what you're saying now is, well, unfathomable. I'd say life's been pretty good for you—and me—and it will continue to be if you just keep moving forward. And look for the positive, my friend, the positive!

Sufficiencius: How I wish I could. But the trends—

Utilitarius: Excuse me. Before you launch into your next rant, let me take a completely different cut at your question.

Sufficiencius sat back, took a deep breath, and gazed out a window. Restraint is a virtue, he told himself. Then he turned to Utilitarius.

Sufficiencius: Okay, what's your new cut on "the environment"? I do hope this one is more ecological.

Utilitarius: I think so. It's about the climate. That's pretty ecological, wouldn't you say?

Sufficiencius: Sure.

Utilitarius: Okay. I'll assume that the climate is changing (it always has, you know) and that ice sheets are melting and sea levels are rising. These are serious threats.

Sufficiencius: All right! Finally you're talking sense.

Utilitarius: If they're serious threats, we should treat them as such.

Sufficiencius: That's right!

Utilitarius: We need to all come together, agree on a plan of action, spare no resources, financial, human, or technological, urge our leaders to act forcefully, support them fully, and attack the problem.

Sufficiencius: Uh, well . . . That sounds like a battle plan, actually, a military campaign.

Utilitarius: Yeah, so? When there are threats to life and liberty, you prepare to defend yourself. In some cases, you don't wait for the worst, you attack preemptively.

Sufficiencius: Uh, yeah, but . . .

Utilitarius: Not getting squeamish, are you? It's a serious threat, right?

Sufficiencius: Yes, but . . . but . . .

Sufficiencius needed a moment to think. He walked out the door while Utilitarius sat staring out the other window. Sufficiencius came back, still frowning.

Sufficiencius: Who is the enemy?

Utilitarius: What do you mean?

Sufficiencius: You outlined a battle plan against environmental threats. Who's the enemy?

Utilitarius: Well, the climate.

Sufficiencius: Let me see if I've got this right. If the climate is being disrupted, it's a threat to us. And like with all threats to our well-being—threats from our enemies, criminals—we have to defend ourselves. Sometimes we even have to attack. Is that right?

Utilitarius: Yes, you got it. Congratulations!

Sufficiencius: No, actually what I got is one bizarre idea: the environment is a threat to humans.

Utilitarius: Yeah, so? You asked for an ecological example. It's a dangerous world out there. Nice talk and chummy cooperating isn't going to cut it when threats are serious.

Sufficiencius: Did it ever occur to you that "the threat" might be us? When scientists document one trend after another of ecological loss, of degradation, of irresistible decline, they see the enemy, and it is *us*!

Utilitarius: Cute. Pogo, right?

Sufficiencius: Right. I thought you'd like that reference—from your era.

Utilitarius: I do, but cartoons aren't the real world. Cartoonists can point fingers all they want; they don't have to make tough decisions.

Sufficiencius: Tough decisions like choosing paper or plastic?

Utilitarius: Are you being sarcastic again?

Sufficiencius: Yes. In your world, consumers keep on buying while leaders and their armies protect oil supplies. Where does nature come in? Where do ecosystems come in? Where do the essential cycles of nutrients and water and life itself come in? I just can't understand how you view such things as "the enemy."

Utilitarius: Well, now. First, as for tough decisions, I mean meeting next month's payroll, balancing a budget, fighting crime, defending ourselves against foreign aggressors. Second, as I told you, I like the environment as much as the next guy.

Sufficiencius: But you're liking it to death! You and your kind have got to, as you said, ease up. Ease up on the cutting and mining and consuming. Ease up on all the waste. Ease up on this manic growth machine, this planetary Frankenstein's monster. Don't you see that?

Utilitarius: What I see is a nice boy who's become one angry fellow.

Sufficiencius: When I see needless destruction and waste, lost lives and livelihoods for millions, even billions of people, now and in the future, not to mention extinct species and despoiled land and water, I get angry. I—

Utilitarius: Listen. We agreed to avoid making this personal. Since you don't seem to like the way I view things, despite all the peace and prosperity such thinking has brought, why don't you tell me how *you* view things, and we'll leave it at that. Okay?

Sufficiencius: Okay, fair enough. So here's how I see things.

Utilitarius: In a nutshell. I have a plane to catch.

Sufficiencius: Sure. "The environment" is, like I said, similar to a life-support system on a spaceship—a system essential to life, hopefully resilient (it can adapt to new circumstances), but unavoidably fragile, too. "The environment" is also like our skin. When astronauts look at the blue dot in space, they sometimes remark that only the layer at the surface is living. Did you know that most of the life in the soil is found in the top ten centimeters?

Utilitarius: No, I didn't. But how 'bout you skip the biology lesson and keep to your view of the environment?

Sufficiencius: Okay, but my point is that the planet's thin skin of life, like our skin, can be scratched and dried out and even burned, but only so much. After that, we die.

Utilitarius: Okay, okay. I got it. What else?

Sufficiencius: "The environment" is like a homestead, largely self-sufficient, yet dependent on the whims of nature and on one's fellow homesteaders.

Utilitarius: Okay, maybe before industrialization, but not now.

Sufficiencius: Yes, now. All the machines in the world can't remove our dependence on fertile soil, clean, free-flowing water, and breathable air.

Utilitarius: You're sounding like a shrill environmentalist again, just preaching. What else?

Sufficiencius: I'm talking about basics, about ecological, biophysical grounding. On a homestead, you don't eat the seed corn. You don't kill the brood stock. You don't put all your eggs in one basket.

Utilitarius: All good fiscal policies, even today. But like I said, maybe back then, when everyone was a farmer.

Sufficiencius: No, *now*. And in the future, when many more of us, I predict, will be farmers of one sort or another. Besides, we all eat, so we're all part of the food system, part of the culture of agriculture.

Utilitarius: Nice turn of phrase. Still, the homestead metaphor just doesn't work for me.

Sufficiencius: All right, I understand.

Utilitarius: So is that it?

Sufficiencius: No, I have two more.

Utilitarius: Are they really necessary? I think I got your point.

Sufficiencius: Yes, they are necessary. The first one you'll like, I think.

Utilitarius: Okay, try me. But remember, I have a plane to catch.

Sufficiencius: The environment is like a banking system.

Utilitarius: What? You're kidding, right? I was almost getting into your let's-all-love-nature-and-go-back-to-the-land spiel.

Sufficiencius: Actually, that's not the view I just gave you. I don't think you were listening carefully. I said the environment is like—

Utilitarius: All right, all right. Whatever. Tell me how the environment is like a banking system. This I gotta hear.

Sufficiencius: A banking system is made up of many actors—depositors, lenders, traders, a central bank, and various regulators. Right?

Utilitarius: Well, you missed a few things, but go on.

Sufficiencius: The system is mediated by money. And the price of money—the interest rate—is key.

Utilitarius: Okay.

Sufficiencius: There are regulations regarding insider trading, reserve funds, and the like.

Utilitarius: Yes, far too many.

Sufficiencius: But some regulations are necessary, I think you'll agree, to maintain the very foundation of the system.

Utilitarius: Which is what?

Sufficiencius: Trust. Confidence. Everybody's belief that the system works, that if you put money in, you can get it out, that no one has an unfair advantage, that the currency is stable and a dollar is a dollar.

Utilitarius: Yep. You got that right.

Sufficiencius stopped. He looked out one window, then the other. He glanced back at Utilitarius, then continued.

Sufficiencius: Trust is like the integrity of life systems, of organisms, communities, ecosystems. It's hard to put a finger on it, hard to measure—in fact, it's probably impossible to measure. But everyone knows it's essential. It's the glue that holds it all together. With "the environment," one can never take ecological integrity for granted, any more than one can take trust in finance for granted. Each has to be maintained, guarded, protected.

Utilitarius: You mean regulated.

Sufficiencius: That's part of it. Central bankers regulate monetary supply just as timber owners manage a forest or a forest agency manages harvest practices.

Utilitarius: Again, far too much if you ask me.

Sufficiencius: Well, maybe. But ask the employees and investors of those big banks and automakers that went belly-up. Ask the employees and citizens of logging communities devastated by cut-and-run timber companies. Ask—

Utilitarius: I got your point. Go on. I've got to go soon.

Sufficiencius: I know. This is crucial, though, so bear with me. It's not just regulation of investors and loggers that's necessary to maintain trust and integrity in these systems. It's self-regulation. Every player must have reason to restrain oneself, to not "game" the system, to avoid taking advantage of others.

Utilitarius: Sounds good. But there's this thing called "human nature." People cheat.

Sufficiencius: Yes, they do. But people also organize themselves and set up rules to minimize cheating and maximize trust or integrity. They manage their reputations. We've seen it in the financial system, at least since the Great Depression—until recently. Now we need it in ecosystems, in the climate system, in food systems.

Utilitarius: Listen. I'd love to chat further about your ideas, strange as they are, but I really have to go.

Sufficiencius: Just one more.

Utilitarius: Make it quick.

Sufficiencius: The environment is a gift.

Utilitarius: Huh?

Sufficiencius: Yes, a gift. Not something we buy at a store; not an endless frontier of endless exploitation, not a lab of freewheeling experiments, but a gift. "The environment" is given to us, to use but not to abuse. We don't own it and we aren't owed it. And like in all giving, we give back; we nourish the environment as it nourishes us.

Utilitarius: Okay, okay. I was almost with you on the banking example. But I'll leave the mushy stuff to lovers and philosophers. Gotta go.

Sufficiencius: All right. Have a good trip.

Sufficiencius got on his bicycle and rode back down the hill to his home.

Language matters. Not just words and phrases, but the underlying concepts and ideas. Among the most significant are metaphors. And what matters is not just the choice of terms, but the choice of what's important.

I had long thought metaphors were for poets and novelists and overwrought journalists. Since I hated eighth-grade English class (and, come to think of it, high school and college English classes, too), metaphors were not for me.

Then I came upon the work of cognitive linguist George Lakoff, linguistic philosopher Mark Johnson, and others. Drawing on their fields plus neuroscience, evolutionary biology, psychology, and so on, they show that metaphors are embodied; they connect how we perceive with what we believe. They help establish a worldview that guides not just how we *see* our environment, but how we *relate to* our environment. Or as philosopher Erazim Kohák put it, "A metaphor is a mask that molds the wearer's face."[1]

So metaphors are more than rhetorical or poetic flourishes. Indeed, although "metaphor has traditionally been viewed as a matter of mere language," write Lakoff and Johnson, cognitive science indicates that it is best understood "as a means of structuring our conceptual system and the kinds of everyday activities we perform." What is more, Lakoff and Johnson argue, "it is reasonable enough to assume that words alone don't change reality. But changes in our conceptual system do change what is real for us and affect how we perceive the world and act upon those perceptions."[2] The two worlds of Utilitarius and Sufficiencius are real. Neither is necessarily "right." But how the two conceptualize "the environment," what metaphors they use, does matter—a lot—especially for the purpose of designing policies, educating the young (and old), and structuring people's lives with analogies and images and expectations. Indeed, metaphors are devices for establishing a society's norms and principles, from which we get rules and procedures, laws and regulations.

Metaphors guide action appropriately to the extent that they are grounded in experience, direct and indirect, and fit the purpose at hand. In Utilitarius's day, it was building a great nation, spurring a vibrant economy, extending freedoms to distant lands. In Sufficiencius's day, it is reversing the negative trends and getting on a sustainable path, living with a lot less material and energy, structuring our lives from the local to the global as if we indeed have this one and only planet.

The fact that metaphors are inescapable, that they provide normative interpretations and affect how we act, suggests that new metaphors, *ecologically grounded* ones, can indeed be made. They can be tools for imagining and enacting an ecological order. The fundamental shifts now under way require such tools. They help us shift away from a view of the environment as store, machine, colony, laboratory, and enemy toward something more like a life-support system, the thin skin of life, a homestead, a banking system, or even a gift. (See Box 10.1.) They help construct new worldviews: the topic of the next chapter.

Box. 10.1
Metaphors of the environment

We need metaphors of the environment as tools for living well and well within our means, for constructing an "a home economy." They should be at once ecological, adaptive, and oriented to complex systems and the far future. Here are some nominations. I have generated the first ten, and the rest have been offered by students, colleagues, energy officials, and others. None are perfect (metaphors never are), but hopefully they are suggestive of the kind of language needed.[1]

- Spaceship Earth (a fragile life-support system)
- Planet Earth (limits to growth)
- A watershed (always an upstream and a downstream)
- Seed that must be saved (restraint in consumption across time makes sense)
- A scale (in balance, right-sized)
- The tide (ebb and flow, cyclic, renewing)
- A network (complex and with emergent properties)
- A homestead (crops, shelter, neighbors)
- A gift (precious, nonproprietary)
- The national banking system (depends ultimately on trust)
- A garden
- A mother (nature)
- A pendulum
- A host (in a symbiotic relationship)
- A nest
- A playground
- A body
- A lifeboat/houseboat
- An island
- A rechargeable battery
- An olive grove
- A sanctuary

11

To Sustainabilize: The Adaptive Strategy of Worldviews

Some 150 years ago, the United States of America set about to industrialize. The challenge was not just to build factories, hire workers, and produce goods. Rather, it was to get an entire nation to *think* like industrialists. Not everyone had to *be* industrialists. There would still be farmers and teachers and preachers. But everyone had to adopt the worldview of the industrialists, including the farmers and the teachers and the preachers.

The challenge was enormous. Some 85 percent of the U.S. population was still rural; people worked a small plot of land or managed a dry goods store or bartered furs and gunpowder. Industrialists, a tiny fraction of that population, needed workers, meaning that people had to abandon their accustomed ways, even their land and shops. For this, early industrialists changed the rules of the game, writing laws to favor big manufacturing and disfavor small proprietorships. Most significantly, though, they created a *new language*—not just new words, but new concepts, new ways of seeing and understanding and valuing the world. Among them were "efficiency," "progress," "modern," and "consumer." And it worked. Society industrialized. It didn't just build steel plants and railroads and assembly lines; it adopted a whole new way of thinking, of seeing the world, indeed, of *creating* a world. And all from scratch, all from a few ideas, a vision, a compelling need, and the will to promulgate it all.

The challenge today is, shall we say, to "sustainabilize."[1] It is no less difficult than the challenge 150 years ago. To be clear, though, the goal now is not to deindustrialize or reindustrialize, any more than the goal then was to de-agrarianize or re-agrarianize. Back then the objective was not to modify rural life or to make marginal changes in agrarian social structure. Rather, early industrialists envisioned an entirely new social order, one unimaginable to all but a few (and even those few could not quite have imagined what actually materialized). It was an order compelled by circumstance—the need to settle a continent, to rebuild after a devastating civil war, to create a great power, to feed a hungry nation. And it was an order compelled by opportunity—a wealth of natural resources, endless frontiers, science, and boundless entrepreneurship.

It was a stupendous achievement, literally a radical new social order. Centuries-old practices were overturned, called old-fashioned, backward, or quaint. The new normal generated untold wealth and power. It did, in short, instill an entirely new worldview, drawing on elements of the existing one. Both farmers and bankers would stimulate growth, for example. But now national greatness would be perceived through machines and markets, all conceived as progress and destiny.

Can a similar transformation occur today? Given the human pressures on basic biophysical systems, can we "sustainabilize"? We too are compelled by circumstance—the need to stabilize the climate, to achieve a steady-state economy, to live within our means. But now, unlike in the past, abundant resources and empty waste sinks cannot be assumed. Rather, the challenge now is one of restraint, of restricting others' attempts to displace costs, of defining the good life as something other than the consuming life. The challenge now is stemming the growth in material things while promoting growth in nonmaterial things.

So, yes, the challenge is fundamentally different now, but it always is fundamentally different at the dawn of a new era. Some will cling to the industrial worldview and seek answers in more efficient technologies and greener markets. In fact, that is the prevailing approach to climate change. With it comes not just the familiar, the same patterns of working and spending (only "greener," of course), but the same structures of power and means of exchange. Others will turn to environmentalism. Whether seen as a movement, a loose collection of activist organizations, a set of laws, treaties, and regulations, or some combination thereof, the essence of environmentalism is

1. a view of the world (the natural world is being degraded by humans);

2. a position (the degradative trends must be reversed);

3. a conversion strategy (those who accept tenets 1 and 2 must convert those who do not).

It is tenet 3 that should trouble us. Proselytizing is for religions (maybe). At one level, no one has to be convinced that clean water, clean air, healthy food, and a stable climate are good things. And no one wants a group of self-appointed experts, true believers, and nature lovers to proclaim that they are the smart, knowledgeable, and correct ones, implying that all others are stupid, ignorant, and wrong. Aside from the arrogance of it all, it is strategically deficient: proselytizing engenders resentment, and from resentment comes backlash, clever misbehavior, and denial, if not totalitarian impulses. The preachiness of many environmentalists is born of deep concern for the environment. But it implies that to protect the environment, it is necessary to adopt one correct worldview.

Here I outline a different approach, one that accepts a plurality of worldviews, each of which frames perception and shapes behavior and all of which can adapt to new circumstances. This approach may strike some as revolutionary (which it is) or utopian (which it is not), but the important thing to realize is that this approach is no more revolutionary or utopian than the work of the early industrialists. What I intend it to be is an adaptive strategy, a tool for sustainabilizing. It says, in effect: if your environment is undesirable, or if it is changing in threatening ways, here's how we, our community, and our nation can adjust; here's how we can change that environment, whether biophysically or socially or both, and how it will likely change us in the process. Here is a set of worldviews, each coherent and intelligible on its own terms, each a source of tactics in a strategy of adaptation to one's environment; we can draw from them as we see fit.

Worldviews of the Environment

All humans have worldviews of the environment. For some "the environment" is simply all that is outside one's skin. It may be literally worldwide in scope (say, the astronaut's view of the blue planet) or just that which one perceives in daily life—one's home and neighborhood, place of work and worship, playground and café. For others "the environment" is the natural world, especially the parts that are untrammeled by humans.

Worldviews are indeed views, what we see and what we do not see. Each has an optical range, a perceptual field. In the tropical jungle, we don't see the office towers where people decide to cut the jungle's trees. In the urban jungle, we don't see the tropical forests cut to build our houses and fire our furnaces. So where we stand, which vehicle we climb into, which overlook we stop at, determines what we see. To this extent, worldviews are *chosen*: where we cast our gaze largely determines what we believe exists, what we value, and what we do to construct a livable world. And it is a livable world that our material striving is all about, not just for the present but for the foreseeable future.

As an adaptable organism, one whose temporal scale of adapting ranges from the millennia of biological evolution to the years of the life course to the hours and minutes of the brain's continuous neural reorganization, we humans are not limited to one worldview. We acquire different views from early childhood, unknowingly for the most part, but we change them as conditions require. Even if one worldview is dominant (it's a dog-eat-dog world out there; humans are gregarious and naturally cooperative), we also hold others, and we draw on each as circumstances warrant. So just because the tropical jungle dweller and the urban jungle dweller occupy vastly different worlds, there is no reason to assume their worldviews are incompatible. Transferred from one setting to the other, each can adapt. The two are of the same species, after all, and a highly adaptive one at that. When humans find themselves in different places, whether geographic, cultural, or psychological, they adopt different views. And humans are perfectly capable of *choosing* new viewscapes, especially when new paths are taken that open new vistas, when livelihoods or lives are threatened, or when others see what one has heretofore not seen.[2]

So my premise is that we inhabit our environment in part by finding our place in it, by seeking out favorite peaks and valleys, useful paths and crossings, pleasing climes. We inhabit the world we attend to, said psychologist William James a century ago.[3] And through that attention we also *construct* our environment: we clear brush and soften the soil, we lure prey and cultivate crops, we build shelters and temples, and we gather others around us. How we do all this depends on what environment is in our purview, what combination of trees and fish, rocks and rivers, on the one hand, and people, buildings, and tools, on the other. We can choose to see the Great Industrial Edifice, or we can choose to see a House of Cards. We can adapt to either, or create a different viewscape—say, a Home Economy (chapter 2).

On top of all this, we are well adapted to our chosen environment to the extent that there is consonance between the natural and the social, to the extent that one does not overwhelm the other, as when the natural is foreboding (the woods are dark and evil) or the human degrades the natural (clear-cut forests "flip" into degraded scrub). Humans are well adapted for the long term—that is, their practices are sustainable—when their constructions only *build on* the natural substrate, not *erode* that substrate.

So worldviews are chosen, but not all at once; they are not ready-made. What is chosen is constructed, deliberately fashioned to serve a purpose. Worldviews are the binoculars that connect humans and their sense of self to their surroundings, their environment, their world. With the chambers and lenses of a worldview, we "see" a world literally—that is, visually and through our other senses—and we "see" a world in the sense of understanding it, of making sense of it, of distinguishing what is important and what is not. There is an ethic in every worldview. But like binoculars, telescopes, and microscopes, no single worldview can encompass everything. Some worldviews are telescopic, making distant objects seem near. But these necessarily obscure the near-at-hand. Some worldviews are microscopic, making intelligible that which is so close, so minute, we can hardly see it. And these necessarily obscure the distant. Some worldviews focus sharply on an object, necessarily forfeiting that object's surroundings. And some have a wide range, bringing much into view yet offering little that is clear.

Through the binoculars of worldviews we detect not just location (monoculars do that, too) but also depth and motion. Together we comprehend time, an abstract but highly useful concept (chapter 5). Extrapolating from other personal experiences (pushing a rock to cause it to move; stacking blocks of wood to create a barrier; carving a bowl to carry food) we comprehend, in our worldview, other abstractions, other concepts—for example, power, control, nurturance, numbers. A worldview is thus both physical and conceptual. And because it is necessarily selective, it is normative: it incorporates and expresses values (chapter 6). As a result, the three components of a worldview are *perceptions*, *beliefs*, and *values*.

Regarding perceptions, while all senses contribute to a worldview, some are more important than others. Fish sense water movement with their lateral lines, birds sense updrafts through their feathers, and humans largely sense their surroundings by what they see with their eyes, hear with their ears, and touch with their hands. In this regard, humans differ from other creatures in the sensory organs employed and the relative importance of these organs. Our world is in part what we see and touch, just as a fish's world is in part the water pressures it feels and a bird's world the wind currents it rides. What distinguishes the human are beliefs and values. Our worldview is what we see with our eyes through the chambers of the binoculars and what we manipulate with our hands by directing and focusing those binoculars.

Beliefs are the lens and filters of the binoculars, the concepts that organize and arrange from top to bottom, front to back. They are rooted in our ancestral past, shaped by personal experience, and governed by cultural expectation and sanction. From a human evolutionary and cultural perspective, they are the necessary complement to perceptions: how we perceive was largely laid down in our long-ago past. But we have refined that selection through cognition, through the uniquely human ability to conceptualize. So just as no species perceives everything, no human conceives everything; not all concepts are useful or adaptive. Thus values enter as the third component, the needs and interests the viewer applies using the binoculars or worldviews, the means of selecting what is perceived and conceived.

Values give direction to our physical and social adaptations. They establish the criteria by which we focus our perceptions and build our concepts. They are, in the first instance, about finding food, shelter, and mates, about avoiding predators and diseases, and about coping with precipitous cliffs and treacherous waters. They are also about human association, about nurturance, protection, cooperation, competition, hierarchy. And they are about higher purpose, about finding one's place in the world, about helping others, about building institutions, about personal expression and societal coherence.

In sum, worldviews are about perceiving and conceiving and making sense of one's world. A given worldview, like a given set of binoculars, is designed for a purpose, for one view, one subset of the larger world. Worldviews are inherently and unavoidably constrained in some way—in the focus or the range or the depth of the view. As the purpose of the worldview changes, so do the worldviews. Thus, people have *multiple worldviews*, including conflicting views, and *those views can change*, separately and in combination.

The key behavioral trait in modern society's conversion from endless industrial expansion to an ecological order is *adaptiveness*. An individual or a society is well adapted when (1) its shared collection of worldviews connects to the physical and social environment; and (2) it can shift worldviews as the physical and social environments shift, all to enable people's surviving and thriving.

Four Worldviews of the Environment

In the current industrial, commercial and expansionist order, four worldviews of the environment can be discerned. I will call them naturist, agrarian, mechanistic, and economistic. Each is an "ideal type," a stylized, polar-case construction meant to highlight particular features. And each has a field of view, a focus of attention, a timescale, and a set of archetypal actors.

In the naturist worldview, "the environment" is all about matter and energy and living things, all out there that is "natural," all that would exist whether or not humans exist. The field of view ranges from subatomic particles to the universe. The focus of attention is on knowing this environment, on modeling and explaining physical laws, chemical bonds, organismal development, speciation. The timescale ranges from the lifespan of a quark to the lifespan of a galaxy. Archetypal actors are physicists, chemists, and biologists. Those actors who have cross-cutting focuses—the paleontologists, ecologists, and atmospheric chemists, for example—approximate the knowledge essential to ecological practice. Yet in this ideal type worldview, the focus is not on practice but on knowing, on analyzing, describing, explaining, and predicting the natural world—that is, primarily a nonhuman world.

In the *mechanistic* worldview, the environment is a system of interlocking pieces, of atoms and molecules, land and water, minerals and organisms, tectonic plates and magma, all in place and in motion according to the laws of gravity and thermodynamics and quantum mechanics. As with a machine, the pieces fit together yet can be rearranged. And like a machine, the environment can be rebuilt, made better, and entirely new ones can be built as well. The field of view includes all that can be manipulated, traditionally everything from agricultural plants and animals to rivers and mountains. The focus is on arranging the environment for beneficial human use—that is, intervening and managing. The time frame ranges from hours and days (e.g., food) to decades (e.g., buildings). Archetypal actors are engineers, planners, and architects.

The naturist and mechanistic worldviews of the environment explicitly encompass the natural world (unlike the economistic; see below) and yet are poles apart in their ideals—knowing versus manipulating, understanding pristine nature versus creating a new nature.

The *agrarian* worldview of the environment is, like the mechanistic, interventionist and managerial, yet its knowledge is acquired through practice and for the purpose of enhancing practice—agrarians' own practice and that of their community. Direct interaction with the land—farming, fishing, or logging, for instance—and direct social relations within their residential community are the bases of that knowledge and practice. What's more, that knowledge and practice accrue and evolve over a lifetime and across generations. Like the naturist view, the agrarian view is inherently cross-cutting, even holistic, and long-term. Unlike the naturist, however, and more like the mechanistic, the agrarian view has the goal of resource use, of material provisioning, all for human sustenance.

For the agrarian, consequently, nature is "in here"—in a crop's yield, in a stock animal's birthing, in a fish's attraction to bait. And it operates on a limited scale: its field of view is that of the practice itself, not watersheds or bioregions, let alone the planet, but the farm or the fishery or the timberland. While the naturist worldview aims to be all-encompassing (systemic, universal, sometimes holistic), the "nature" of relevance to the agrarian is only that which can be manipulated and that affects one's harvest—the soil, seed, livestock, sunlight, moisture, ocean bottom. Its focus, therefore, is yield. Archetypal actors are farmers, fishers, and loggers.

The *economistic* worldview of the environment is also one of the material world, but not the entire material universe, only that of human exchange, of producing and consuming. It is products and services that are of interest, not atoms, molecules and energy, let alone living systems. And it is all about transaction, about buying and selling, investing, pricing, retailing, and purchasing. It is, above all, about the clearing of markets and the efficient allocation of resources, physical and human. Its field of view stretches from one side of the input-output model, where raw material enters production, to the other, where wastes exit—that is, from sources to sinks. If either sources or sinks become scarce, rising prices via the market stimulate new sources, new sinks, and substitutes. Its focus, therefore, is price. Its temporal scale is short-term, even instantaneous; it systematically discounts the future (through the "discount rate") and ignores the past. Archetypal actors are economists, planners, policy analysts, and investors.

The economistic worldview of the environment has no natural or ecological component; everything of concern is reducible to money or hypothetical "utiles," and all is substitutable. But its dominance in modern life (along with the mechanistic) warrants inclusion in a framework of worldviews aiming at an ecological order.

The Adaptiveness of Worldviews

These four worldviews of the environment—naturist, mechanistic, agrarian, and economistic—are starting points. They are among the overarching systems of perception, belief, and value from which an individual's and a society's resource behaviors stem. They are not determinative, but they frame perception and shape behavior. They set what is expected—what is normal and what is deviant. And they provide the raw material to build the institutions and the language for major goals such as ecological and social sustainability.

People and especially societies do not have a single, exclusive worldview, though. In the area of environment and natural resources, they are not either naturistic or economistic, mechanistic or agrarian. They have, or have the capacity to have, more than one worldview, to simultaneously draw on one or another as conditions demand. On a newspaper's business page, the economistic worldview prevails. But in the science section, the naturist prevails. Many readers peruse both—and with no conflict.

So we hold *clusters* of worldviews. Circumstances—material, ideational, and cultural/historical factors, or recent experience—determine the predominance of one worldview over another. Significantly, they can *change*, and an existing worldview can be modified—refocused, redirected, or combined.

Worldviews begin to form in early adulthood through a process of acculturation influenced by genetic predisposition.[4] They are resistant to change because they constitute a system, a mostly integrated set of perceptions, beliefs, and values that enable the individual to function in the larger world. But worldviews can adapt to new circumstances and new knowledge if two conditions are met. First is a major perturbation—a life-threatening event, for instance, or a dramatic shift in income. The second is external support, a family or a social institution that reinforces the requisite new perceptions, beliefs, and values.

To illustrate, imagine that an engineer worked all his professional life on the levees surrounding New Orleans. He measured and calculated constantly, supervising new construction and maintenance. He long advocated Category 3, even Category 4 hurricane protection. He firmly believed that whatever the weather event, a levee system could be built to withstand the forces of nature. And he knew that his work was an important contribution to such a system. Then along comes Hurricane Katrina. After the shock of all the destruction and after new calculations he comes to the conclusion that no levee system can be as foolproof as he once thought. In fact, after talking to numerous ecologists and hydrologists and joining the Society of Ecological Engineers, he now firmly believes that the only way to protect New Orleans is to reconsider the channeling of the Mississippi River upriver and the draining of the delta downriver; in other words, he now sees that protection is an issue of the entire watershed and, with climate change, eventually the entire planet. He still works on the levees, measuring and calculating; it's what he does; it is his work. But he now views his world differently. He has shifted from a predominantly mechanistic worldview of the environment to one that includes a naturist worldview.

So what shifts are most useful to the goal of an ecological order, to sustainable practice? As much as some sustainability proponents would like to see a wholesale societal conversion to a completely new worldview grounded in, say, the naturist worldview (especially its cross-cutting ecological variant) or to the agrarian (especially the food-growing variant that challenges industrial agriculture), a premise here is that the economistic and mechanistic are too deeply embedded in modern industrial societies. Moreover, although the economistic and mechanistic may appear completely antithetical to the goal of ecological sustainability, each has elements compatible with the naturist and agrarian. The key analytic task is not to pick the winning view but to specify the criteria by which the elements of existing views are selected for decision making and institutional design. Because our fundamental concern is diminished ecological capacities, the selection criteria must be rooted in the biophysical, the ecological, and these, it turns out, are best represented by the naturist and the agrarian.

How, then, would the economistic worldview contribute to a sustainability worldview? Consider finance, a subset of economic activity where there are time-honored maxims to counter the human tendencies to overspend, to put all one's eggs in the same basket, to draw down one's account, to spend now, pay later. These tendencies and the problems they generate for the individual and society are analogous to drawing down a natural resource, harvesting as if there was no tomorrow, killing the brood stock, eating the seed corn. The following financial maxims are thus analogous to ecological imperatives:

- Spend within one's means.
- Diversify the portfolio.
- Draw on the interest, not the principal.
- Balance the budget.

To illustrate, investors know well the wisdom of having a diversified stock portfolio. So do community and national planners: single-product economies are inherently unstable, prone to collapse when consumer preferences shift, capital moves elsewhere, the economy takes a dive, or new technologies replace the product. Imagine the dependency of a company town that produces one thing, such as lumber, by one company or a country that exports one commodity, such as oil or bananas. But just as economic diversity protects investments and jobs, ecological diversity protects the natural resource base. Applying a diversification principle to agriculture, for example, would raise serious questions about the wisdom of monoculture farms that cover vast acreages or plantation timbering with ever shorter rotations. Applying a spend-the-interest-only principle to groundwater would challenge the tendencies to increase pumping rates regardless of recharge and to search for "new sources" of water.

As a subset of the economistic worldview, then, the field of view of the financial is expansive yet includes only that which can be monetized (through risk, probabilities, and payments). Its focus is security.[5] Its temporal scale can be very long, as much as decades, even centuries (witness Lloyd's of London). Moreover, stability in the financial system is crucial. Confidence and enforceable contracts are essential. Thus, as divorced from the ecological as the financial side of the economistic worldview appears to be, it does offer a way to connect to the more ecological worldviews, the naturist and the agrarian, and hence to the goal of an ecological order.

Other worldviews can be similarly refocused and combined. The crucial first step is to identify segments of the worldview that appear to have ecological and social content, that is, that correspond to identifiable processes and constraints and thus point in the direction of a stable, long-term ecological order. The next step is to combine two or more such segments and derive principles and metaphors for sustainability. For example, the naturist view has an inherent notion of limits, whether of energy (the laws of thermodynamics) or of ecosystems (a range of operation beyond which the system "flips") or of individuals (a range of temperature and water tolerances). The agrarian has a notion of husbandry (caring for natural elements so as to supply human necessities) and cycling (crops need rotating, animals need rest). These two notions lead to principles of sufficiency (don't push natural and social systems to the extreme) and intermittency (build in down time for reproduction and recuperation) (chapter 5), along with the metaphor of a life-support system, taken from emergency health care and spaceship design (chapter 10).

In short, this nonexclusive, pluralist, and dynamic approach to worldviews is one way of saying that individuals and societies are, or can be, *adaptive*, that what worked in one era (localized husbandry in the agricultural period; expansion in the age of exploration; mechanistic reasoning in industrialization; economistic reasoning in the commercial, consumerist period) can shift in another era, in one driven, for instance, by biophysical constraint. Moreover, it suggests that many worldviews of the environment, not just the naturist or agrarian, say, are potential sources of organizing principles and language for sustainable practice. It is the *shift in worldviews,* supported by institutions and language, by social organizing principles and metaphors, that leans behavior *away from mining and toward sustaining.*

No One Right View

"The environment" has never been just another issue area represented by another interest group. "The environment" is the very material substrate on which all else rests, on which all human constructions are built. It is the grand biophysical system that contains and supports and sets limits on lesser subsystems (e.g., the economy). It is that thin skin of life that constantly grows and decays, constantly adapts to the interactions of organisms and their nonliving world. It is, on this spaceship called Planet Earth, the life-support system we all depend on. It is at once resilient and fragile.

To shore up this base, to keep human activity within bounds, to adapt fast enough but not too fast, to maintain the life-support apparatus, no single view of the environment can be "the right view," the one and only way, the received wisdom that all others must bow to, the enlightenment that all others must acquire, the religion to which all must convert. With current knowledge of the current state of flux (political, economic, cultural), no one can say a priori what that new set of worldviews, the "sustainability" worldviews, would be. Rather, all we can do, all people have ever done when confronted with crisis and the need for fundamental change, is move in a new direction, chart a new course, clear a new path, and do so by drawing on what we already have, what we already know, including the perceptions, beliefs and values—that is, the worldviews—we already have. Yes, new ones are likely to emerge, but we're not there yet.

So existing worldviews must illuminate the new path at the same time the very character of the problem—the need to reverse the trends in environmental degradation and live within immutable ecological, social, and cognitive constraints—points the way. To establish that path is to plot coordinates given not by the stars, not by machines that spin continuously and can always be repaired, not by laboratories that can confidently seal off a messy outer world, and certainly not by a vision of endless growth, benign metastasizing of one species' metabolism inside that larger body called the biosphere. Rather, it is to take its coordinates from those processes that define the very issue at hand—namely, thermodynamics, solar flux, nutrient cycling, ecosystem functioning, evolutionary adaptation, reproduction, collective action, cognition—all in the human context of practice, of good work, of restraint.

It is a difficult course, a path full of unknowns, but in some sense a rather simple one, too: humans are the quintessential adaptive creature. We have adapted to constraints and dramatic change before, some physical, some social, but each novel in its time. There is every reason to believe that we can do it again. Yes, global ecological constraint is novel, but living on one plot of land, drawing from one limited-flow river, harvesting from one forest and one fishery has been done before, repeatedly, all over the world, across cultures and across time. And, arguably, a whole lot of it has been done over very long periods of time—in other words, sustainably.

How humans have done this before depended greatly on how they perceived our environment (Is it "out there" or "in here"? Are humans a part of the environment or apart from it?), how they believed it works (Are the natural resources potentially renewing? Can other users be excluded?), and how they valued it (Is it for immediate monetary gain or for long-term sustenance?). In short, whether we mine or sustain depends in large part on our view of the environment.

To presume otherwise, to presume that there is a correct view of the environment, is to presume that some people have that view and all others do not and thus that the charge of the knowing is to enlighten the unknowing, to convert them by education or fear or bribe ("incentive").

The approach taken here is far less proselytizing, far less arrogant and presumptuous. It assumes that the raw materials—the perceptions, beliefs, and values—already exist, that they can be found in some of the unlikeliest places (e.g., finance), that a good many people already have the requisite perceptions, beliefs, and values, even if they do not fit the nature-loving, eco-centric, postmodern profile. Think of the trekkers in chapter 2, exploring and listening, or the good work of other characters in previous chapters. In fact, if these four worldviews are close to being comprehensive—that is, if together they encompass a large proportion of a contemporary industrialized society—they constitute prima facie evidence for the claim that the raw materials for an ecological order already exist; little has to be created de novo, few people have to be converted, little by way of rewards and punishments must be concocted.

And maybe most important of all, the adaptive approach taken here assumes that the requisite change, the willingness to sustainabilize, is most likely to succeed not when people are preached to, made fearful, bribed, and coerced, but when they themselves can experiment, create, and solve their own immediate problems. It is most likely when people can connect their local problem solving to the larger global problem solving. What's more, this approach is *inherently* democratic; it requires widespread networks of participation and meaningful decision making; it eschews elite, top-down, command-and-control, incentive-driven approaches. It demands that leaders not command but support.

The "adaptive person" approach deriving from multiple worldviews is not just respectful of different views, not just more participatory and democratic; it also conforms with what we know about human behavior, individual and collective, that makes for healthy individuals and communities. That is, humans are at their best when

1. they are faced with a genuine challenge;

2. they are creative and productive;

3. they find meaning in their own problem solving and in acts larger than themselves;

4. they help themselves and help others;

5. they self-organize and self-govern;

6. they feel they are getting a fair shot at the benefits of their work.

We are the quintessential adaptive creature, and adaptive in two senses. One is primarily physical, involving features such as our brain and eyes, our upright gait, our ability to speak. We all have these features, and they pass from generation to generation. The other is the capacity to adapt to new and changing environments during one's lifetime. Our brain is not just an adaptation acquired during the hunter-gatherer stage to function in that ancestral environment. It is also an *adapting organ*, one that constantly adjusts to its environment—the body, immediate others, and the larger world, biophysical and social. The mind is both *adapted* and *adapting*.[6]

So the capacity to construct a worldview is an adaptation that probably goes back to the Pleistocene, those 2 million years that largely shaped us into the organism we are today. But a given worldview for a given individual is the product of an adapting mind: a mind that from birth is constantly building its neural pathways to cope with its environment; an environment that, from the individual's perspective, is constantly changing, even in a stable society. That adapting mind is looking for ways of perceiving, of understanding, of separating the important from the less important. In short, it is constantly constructing a worldview, and doing so to meet its needs, to acquire resources, to protect itself, to reproduce, to associate with others, to feel competent and useful, to do good work, to have meaning.

In sum, worldviews are adaptations—adaptive and adapting. They enable us to be a special kind of creature. In a sense, we like adapting (assuming the uncertainties and risks are not overwhelming); it is what we do. We can hardly help but be creative, help ourselves and help others, and assemble teams, all to tackle problems and solve them.

So now, in the twenty-first century, "the world" is changing: a predictable climate is becoming erratic; the cornucopia of goods can no longer be presumed "good," not for everyone, not for the long term; economies dependent on cheap fuels, cheap labor, and clever cost displacement must rebuild fundamentally; the politics of exploitation and domination and dumping necessarily must give way to one of self-determination, risk minimization, and prudence. Now is the time to embrace adaptation, not ever more technological fixes and political gimmicks, let alone more production and consumption, however green. Now is the time for adaptation to a worldview consonant with the world that we have created and that creates us, a world at once threatening and full of new opportunities and new challenges, precisely what can bring out the best in humans.

The operative term in this optimistic conclusion is "can." We can rise to the occasion and create a sustainable and just order, or we can flounder and fight and waste yet more resources, natural and human. It is too easy to say the difference is in the choices we make. The real difference precedes choice; it is in the framing of problems and their solutions, in what we see, what we speak of, and what we value—that is, in worldviews. It is also in finding realistic bases of hope, our final topic.

12

The New Normal

Environmental scholars endure an occupational hazard. The more we learn, whether in the library or lab, at the field site or from the satellite feeds to our computers, the more we come face to face with an inexorable logic of gloom and doom:

• The more we know about environmental trends, the worse things look.

• The worse things look, the greater our responsibility to inform the public.

• To inform the public, we have to tell it like it is, which, to ourselves and others, sounds like gloom and doom.

• The more we talk gloom and doom, the more we chart the trends, the worse things look, the more we are compelled to talk gloom and doom.

• The more we talk gloom and doom, the more gloomy and unhopeful we feel.

For a long time I thought this occupational hazard was unique to our profession and, in particular, to our status as researchers and teachers and writers. But as students, audience members, and friends have conveyed to me over the years, the hazard is not ours alone. People everywhere are concerned, worried, even depressed, and rightfully so. A fundamental shift is under way, and people everywhere sense it.

To break the vicious cycle of gloom and doom, I have come to understand (after much teeth gnashing and whining and sulking of my own), is to face up to three simple truths:

1. A gloom-and-doom approach does not work.

2. There are major forces of extraction and consumption and disposal at work that effectively promote the notion that more is better, normal, even patriotic.

3. There is a fantasy pervading the land that says the planet, aided by clever technologies and well-functioning markets, can withstand yet more abuses, more mining, more consuming, more disposing; we just have to do it better.

So what to do?

First I wish to tell one last story. This is another story about normalcy: the normalcy of smoking. The reader may recall the first story of normalcy, slavery (chapter 4). Historically speaking, the shifts in smoking and slavery are recent transformations from what was perfectly normal to what is now perfectly abnormal. These shifts depended not on gloom and doom but on good research and gutsy people willing to take on some powerful actors, and to do so for many years. What's more, coordinated action made the difference, not changes in individual consumer choice, not technological gimmicks.

From Normal to Abnormal

For much of the twentieth century, smoking was not just acceptable but cool, hip, the thing to do. It was a "cultural icon of sophistication, glamour and sexual allure," as Dr. Howard Markel, professor of pediatrics, psychiatry, and the history of medicine at the University of Michigan put it in a book review.[1] It was even promoted as health-giving. "More doctors smoke Camels than any other cigarette," proclaimed one magazine advertisement in the mid-twentieth century. And I am guessing that many readers of this book can well remember how, in offices and restaurants across the country, people lit up whenever and wherever they wanted. If nonsmokers didn't like it, they could move (after the smokers gave them that "you prude" look). I grew up in a household where both parents smoked. My brother was asthmatic, and it never occurred to my parents—or, apparently, to the family doctor—that smoking might be a contributing factor. Some years earlier my father had jumped out of a DC-3 plane behind enemy lines in Normandy, his smokes safely tucked in his pack, supplied free by some cigarette company. Humphrey Bogart and Miles Davis and virtually everyone else on the big screen and on record albums smoked. Smoking was, for a good century or more, perfectly normal.

Then something funny happened on the way to universal smoking bliss. In odd laboratories around the country a few researchers questioned the normalcy, the conventional wisdom, the health-giving assumptions of smoking. Unlike the industry's researchers, who, "by asking narrow questions and responding to them with narrow research . . . provided precisely the cover the industry sought," says Dr. Allan M. Brandt, a medical historian at Harvard University, these upstart researchers asked the hard questions. They were, of course, attacked by industry, vilified in the press, and denounced by all who smoked or saw the practice as an expression of personal freedom. Even if there were dangers, industry asserted, everyone knew the risks, so smoking was an issue of individual choice and personal responsibility, not corporate responsibility. But the upstart researchers kept asking the hard questions. They did the studies, hard as it was to procure the funding. And the answers they got were hard to disseminate because few wanted to hear them. But then the U.S. surgeon general announced in 1964 that cigarettes caused cancer. He and his successors denounced industry for its self-serving, unscientific claims. They challenged doctors' reassurances and the media's complicity. And they did not fall for the clever technological adjustments to the cigarette—menthol, filters, "low tar"—the tobacco technologists cooked up. They took heat for it, of course; it wasn't easy.[2]

Along the way, the language of smoking changed. "Cool" and "normal" and "free choice" gave way to "cancer-causing" and "secondhand smoke" and "addictive." The industry was exposed for its deliberate distortion of the science, its knowledge of nicotine's addictive qualities, and its marketing (estimated at $15.1 billion in 2003), including special techniques aimed at hooking youth. Now smokers are banished to specially ventilated cages and to outdoor smoking zones well away from children and fellow workers. In short, what was normal and terribly harmful—something that caused over 400,000 deaths in the United States each year (more than HIV, alcohol, illicit drugs, suicide, and homicide combined)—became abnormal.[3] "A conclusion that seems obvious today," writes Dr. Markel, "took most of a century to reach."[4]

Obvious, normal, just the way things happen. Or not. As it stands now, "normal" with respect to fossil fuels is this: burn every last hydrocarbon and pray that, unlike with nuclear waste, we will find places to put vast quantities of carbon dioxide, and those places will be secure for generations to come. "Normal" is to believe such storage is possible despite the lack of any geologic or technological precedent. It is also to believe that if it doesn't work, something else will, so we don't need to worry about this simple fact: the amount of fossil fuels humans have burned to date has, by all indications, disrupted the climate, and there are many times that amount still available in the earth.[5] Slavery and smoking were horrendous, but the consequences of playing out this global gamble are beyond imagination. Burning fossil fuels must become abnormal, subject to capping at zero net emissions like all other life-threatening substances, and condemned as immoral.

Recall that when a few people acquire new understandings, take a strong moral stance, and confront power, things do change. Fundamental shifts have happened before, so they are possible. There is nothing normal about risking the very habitability of the planet. There is nothing normal or inevitable about unending growth on a finite planet. There is nothing normal or inevitable about how a tiny fraction of the world's population holds the bulk of its wealth while a billion or two struggle just to survive from one day to the next. There is nothing normal or inevitable about knowingly degrading ecosystems, permanently extinguishing entire species, or dislocating millions of people by causing sea levels to rise. And there is nothing normal or inevitable about justifying all this in the name of "economic growth" or "progress" or "efficiency" or "jobs" or "return on investment" or "global competitiveness."

So smoking was a story of normal to abnormal in the twentieth century. Slavery was such a story in the eighteenth and nineteenth centuries. And before that there was piracy and blood sports and the Roman circus. The story of the *twenty-first* century is a *fundamental shift*—away from incessant filling of waste sinks and depleting of natural capital and toward fertile soil; clean, free-flowing water; genetic diversity in crops and wildlife; and cultural diversity in peoples and communities. The story of the twenty-first century is living within our means, biophysical and social. It is treading softly on a land that can't take much more. Normal has been believing that consumers rule, that efficiencies will reduce consumption, that green products and convenient choices are quite enough to reverse the trends. They are not, no more than the belief that labels on cigarettes would check nicotine addiction, that better-designed shackles would solve the problems of slave trading. To overcome the gloom and doom of global warming and declining oil and persistent toxics and floods and droughts and wildfires, concerned citizens have to go beyond easy, quick fixes and business as usual. They have to reject the old normal.

To overcome the gloom and doom (and, I have to admit, I just engaged in some), concerned citizens have to actively imagine the possible. This is the basis of hope, *realistic* hope. So I conclude this book with a two-part prescription. The first is to be perfectly aware of the messages and practices around us that sap our energies, that drain our attention, that thwart our creative problem-solving efforts. I will call these *sinks of hope*. (Again, in ecology a "sink" is where wastes go and are eventually assimilated or cycled back through the biosphere.) Sinks of hope are not just receptacles; they are conceptual and rhetorical devices, whether inadvertent or strategic, that draw away hope, that convert the resourcefulness of hope to the despair of hopelessness.

The second prescription is to consciously and realistically build, for oneself and one's community and nation, *sources of hope*. These are tactics that use the tools of previous chapters to effect fundamental change, individual and collective. Together, sinks and sources of hope constitute a "politics" of fundamental change. They are not, though, a complete strategy. Rather, I urge the reader to take these as signposts: some hold warning signs that simultaneously alert a change agent to the risks of business as usual and to the risks of fundamental change; others mount streetlamps that shine light on paths that deviate from "normal" (endless climbing, consuming and disposing, all perilous at a planetary scale). Moreover, I urge the reader to take these signposts not as "the answer," not as a recipe. Instead, readers should find their own paths, however personal, however preliminary and small, against the grade of that endlessly climbing path, the old normal.

Sinks of Hope

Perhaps the surest way to drain hope, others' and one's own, is, as suggested, to preach gloom and doom. This is especially true when no realistic alternative is put forth and when it is accompanied by pleas for good behavior: Please, everyone, throw your recyclables in the designated receptacles. Please! And it is even more true when guilt is the emotional overtone: What's wrong with you? Why can't you see that paper goes in the paper bin, not the trash bin? People are so selfish and thoughtless! Don't they know they're hurting the environment?[6]

A second sink for hope is assuming that the current state of affairs is *normal*, much as smoking was taken as normal for a good century, and slavery before it. This sink finds humans' global ecological predicament to be a perfectly predictable consequence of "human nature." It's a juggernaut. Unstoppable. It's immutable, unreformable. It'll have to spend itself first; a true crisis will have to emerge before things change (chapter 4).

A third sink for hope is using the *language* of maximum economic growth and endless material consumption to promote the very opposite—selective growth for the impoverished, restrained consumption and stabilized economic activity for everyone else. This is like using the language of military conquest to promote peace (we have got to vanquish the foes of cooperation), of dictatorship to promote democracy (we need a strong leader and tough laws to make everyone vote), of mafia tactics to promote the rule of law (severe punishment is the only thing that people understand and that will make them behave right).

A fourth sink for hope is advocating a theory of social change that relies on narrow assumptions about "human nature." One such theory common among scientists is called the "Tragedy of the Commons," where users (cattle grazers on a common meadow or polluters of the ocean) cannot communicate among themselves, cannot restrain their individual tendencies to use more, cannot make commitments to each other, and cannot organize themselves to create rules and enforce them. Curiously, a vast contrary literature exists (which has somehow escaped so many otherwise very scientific people) that indicates that humans are social beings; we are nothing if not creatures who communicate extensively, organize ourselves, and work out rules to live by. Another such theory might be called the "global village." All 6 billion denizens of this world would identify with the world and its problems. Once everyone understands how serious the problems are, they will think globally, act locally, and cooperate to do good for one another. The views of human nature in these two theories of social change are polar opposites—selfishness and altruism—yet both theories are hopelessly (pun intended) idealistic and utopian (or dystopian). The more advocates of these theories run down these paths, the more run down they and their listeners feel.

This is an admittedly depressing list. Before the reader concludes, though, that, yes, this is reality, we are doomed, let's turn to *sources of hope*. And I stress once again that I am flagging *realistic* signs of hope, signs grounded in what people actually can do and what they actually have done. There is nothing Pollyannaish about this list, nothing based on wide-eyed wishful thinking; at least that is what my years of research, practice, teaching, and writing tell me.

This list has two strands—understanding and awareness on the one hand, organizing and politics on the other. It assumes there will be opposition to fundamental change, even personal and professional attack. It is not a list of "easy things you can do to save the planet." Such lists, says political scientist Michael Maniates, "tell us we can change the world through our consumer choices, choices that are economic, simple, even stylish." In light of current crises, he says, "Never has so little been asked of so many at such a critical moment. . . . We're being treated like children by environmental elites and political leaders too timid to call for the best in us or too blind to that which has made us a great nation."[7] The following list, by contrast, is demanding. It treats all of us as citizens first. It takes infinite material growth as impossible, the dream world of those who have never had to pay full freight. It accepts limits; indeed, it embraces them.

Sources of Hope

1   If it exists, it's possible.
This simple maxim was originally propounded by economist and peace scholar Kenneth Boulding. The context then was international conflict, which seemed pervasive, and the "it" was peace. Here the context is excess, and the "it" is living well by living well within our means. If good work and restrained resource use exist, then such practices are possible. Just because they take a backseat in a growth-manic, consumeristic, debt-laden society does not mean they are unrealistic.

One reason this maxim is so powerful is that much about living within our means is indeed *simple*. Not simplistic, not easy and convenient, not stylish, just simple. Consider a town that depends on one underground water supply. If the town's withdrawal exceeds recharge, if the water table consistently drops, its water supply is not sustainable. That's simple. If current consumption patterns worldwide continue, it will require a couple more planets. That's simple. If an economy depends on putting its waste somewhere else and other economies do likewise, pretty soon they are wallowing in one another's waste streams. Displacement of full costs cannot work on a planet full of human activity. That's simple. If a farmer adds more and more acreage, at some point she cannot know the land and all her crops and livestock intimately. She has no choice but to manage by reducing crop diversity and using external inputs like chemical fertilizers. That's simple. I could go on. But I hope the point is clear. For all the sophisticated science done in the name of sustainability, much about living sustainably is really quite simple.

Still, for many of us in high-consuming, easy-money societies, it is hard to imagine living on less. But we need to be clear: the "less" in question is *less than excess*. What's more, the excess of the old normal has depended on huge amounts of readily available cheap energy and vast waste sinks, both of which have appeared to be endless. Boom and bust on a wide-open frontier and expansion across a limitless globe was the norm. But today there are no more frontiers; the planet is full. Full, that is, of human activity and impact. Humans' population (just in my lifetime the population of the United States has doubled), their technology (every acre of land, virtually every drop of freshwater is accounted for), and, yes, their consumption are all well beyond the ecological capacities of the planet. One study after another, on everything from global warming and disappearing species to poisoned waters and depleted soils, from ecological footprints to ever-increasing resource flows, confirms it.

The good news here is that the societies of excess we now consider normal have existed for only a blip in human history. In the vast bulk of history—some fifteen thousand years since early agriculture, maybe longer—humans have been figuring out how to live *with* earth's bounties and *within* its boundaries. For five thousand years Egyptians grew food in the Nile Valley, living *with* the annual flood, not fighting the river by damming and channeling it. Like Edward Abbey (preface), they seem to have found no shortage of water in their desert, but just the right amount. Histories of inshore fisheries, alpine meadows, community forests, private forests, irrigated arid lands, and many more such systems tell the same story: humans are perfectly capable of organizing themselves to limit resource use and sustain the natural bases of their economies. Now, as the waste sinks fill and the cheap oil runs out, we are bound to live sufficiently again. The sooner we adjust, the better. Yes, it will require hard work. But it can be extremely rewarding work, too. Living well within our means has happened before, does happen, and is therefore possible. This is truly a source of realistic hope.

2 Fundamental change always seems impossible before it happens.

There is an old saying: "Before the revolution everyone says it is impossible; after the revolution everyone says it was inevitable." I was a volunteer in the Philippines in the early 1970s. I asked Filipinos why they put up with the horrendous abuses of dictator Ferdinand Marcos. They told me, "You just don't understand the Filipino, Tom. He's not like you Americans. He won't stand up. He just goes along; doesn't want to cause trouble." But a few years later, the so-called people's revolution in Manila toppled Marcos. My Filipino friends then explained that Marcos was horrible; he had to go.

Now, to effect a fundamental shift in how humans connect to the natural world, we hear much the same thing: it is human nature to consume more and more; it is the one and only economy that, above all else, must be protected. Besides, things won't change. People are too entrenched. There's too much power vested in the status quo. That's just the way it is; always has been, always will be. Like that mythical juggernaut that just keeps rolling across the landscape, oblivious to the destruction in its path and (to add a modern gloss) endlessly fueled by carbon molecules and uranium atoms, it is unstoppable. The best we can do is fine-tune it and clean up the mess as it rolls along. But in the long run there is no perpetual motion machine, no beast that consumes voraciously and grows endlessly, no vehicle with endless power running on limitless roads. The contradictions are mounting, the impacts stark, the inequities huge. No amount of industrial inertia, slick green marketing, or efficiencies for efficiency sake can squeeze more life out of this single planet. Times are changing, like it or not, ready or not. Time to get ready, lay some groundwork.

One reason fundamental social change seems impossible is that it typically starts with a few committed people and small acts. As new understandings are acquired (scientific and cultural) and those acts are coordinated to confront the structures of power, change gains momentum. It becomes a movement, not a lifestyle choice. For motive, fundamental change draws on people's basic need for meaning, engagement, and fairness. For perspective, fundamental change toward ecological order draws on worldviews that are grounded. For effectiveness, the shift includes those who are typically excluded, those who involuntarily bear the risks created by those who have the power. We do not so much need a revolution as we need well-defined problems, networks of diverse peoples, and good old hard work. It is possible and it will happen.

3   Solve the right problem.

Old problems prompt old action: growth is necessary, so economic growth must be greened to solve environmental problems; efficiencies can reduce resource use, so all efficiencies must be good for the environment; consumers rule the economy, so they must be persuaded to buy green. New definitions of the problem prompt new action: growth is good *for a purpose* (e.g., to alleviate poverty), so let's grow in the right places, level or reduce resource use elsewhere, and look for quality-of-life improvements where people have grown enough; the efficiency principle leads to unexamined material growth, so let's seek sufficiency, that is, enough and not too much resource use; because consumers buy and citizens act, let's focus on citizen action for real change. And so on. Reframing a problem changes people's thinking, their worldview, and their language, all of which can serve as precursors to fundamental social change.

At the same time, change agents must guard against *diversionary framing*.[8] Common terms and frames—growth, efficiency, consumer demand, equity, for instance—are familiar and can thus seem benign. But they can also perpetuate current trends, whether inadvertently or strategically. With growth, for example, we may think of a child's development, or a corn crop ripening. With efficiency we may think about the avoidance of waste and the satisfaction of a well-tuned engine. With equity we may think about poverty alleviation and democratic representation. But the issue before us and coming generations is *excess*. To paraphrase Herman Daly's lifeboat metaphor, we can load the lifeboat efficiently and fairly, but if we overload it, it will still sink, however efficiently and fairly.[9] The key word is *excess*.

Opponents of fundamental change will select their issues and language carefully. They will divert attention by raising issues of scientific uncertainty, economic impact, consumer choice, personal freedom, technological innovation, jobs, global competition, national security. In such diversions, answers to excess fall to the wayside. Or, as novelist Thomas Pynchon put it: "If they can get you asking the wrong questions, they don't have to worry about the answers."[10] About the answers, in this case, to excess—to an ecological footprint that requires two planets, to soil erosion that wipes out a millennium of buildup, to water withdrawal rates that exceed water recharge rates.

Another common diversion is to claim that *everything must be measured*. Proponents of metrics will say, in effect, that if it can't be counted, it doesn't count; or if it isn't "valued" in the market, we can't know its value; or if it isn't measured, policy makers won't pay attention. Good metrics can certainly help identify trends and measure progress. More emphasis on ecological footprints, greenhouse gas sources, and water depletion rates, and less on gross domestic product, trade flows, and stock market ups and downs would be a good thing. But just as national security, political stability, and constitutional democracy are inherently immeasurable, so are sustainability, food security, and healthy communities. So change agents must be wary of such claims, often implicit in a technological, money-centered society. They should take a measured approach to metrics.

Because the issue at hand is excess, the entire project of living within our means is *normative*. Principles and norms and ethics are central. This is troubling for those who define the problem in terms of technological innovation and market pricing. In academe, business, law, engineering, journalism, and other professions, there is a widespread belief that it is not professional to espouse personal values. According to this viewpoint, professionals just analyze problems (not advocate solutions), promote shareholder value (not other values, because in business "value" means only one thing—money), apply the law (not make the law or shape it or judge it), build what people need (not advocate visions of a manufactured world), and write what happens, not what they would like to see happen. In practice, there are values and moral positions in every act of consequence, individual and collective. Change agents put theirs on the table and demand that the defenders of business as usual do the same. Change agents engage the normative; they don't shy away from it.

So solving the right problem means defining it correctly in the first place. For that, language—ideas, principles, norms, metaphors—is crucial. The language of the new normal has *ecological content* and a *long-term ethic*. The conversation is kept in the territory of fundamentals—the biophysical integrity of water and nutrient cycles, the social integrity of vibrant communities, the life-support investments for future generations. And long time horizons are constantly kept in view when change agents ask, Can this consumption pattern, this development project, this public policy, this financial mechanism be sustained for the indefinite future? For whom? For what purpose?

4   Start on the ground and work up.

There is no single best intervention point; no sector that, if restructured, will create a home economy; no one worldview that will create ecological order. The global environmental problematic is just too complex, encompassing everything from deforestation and toxic substances to freshwater depletion and global warming. It is huge. For those of us who tread this territory day in and day out, it can be overwhelming. But for all that, including every proffered high-technology and market solution, it all comes down to basics—say, to food, water, and energy. If one has a choice of where to intervene, the basics are likely to be where the greatest leverage is in creating a home economy. There the politics of laying groundwork does not align along ideological or ethnic or religious lines. This politics is inherently inclusive, left to right, rich to poor, young to old, white to black. This is not to say that these politics will be easy. Rather, it is to say that the political cleavages of the old normal are likely to smooth out as people create a new normal, as they work hard to procure healthy food, clean water, and renewable energy.[11]

That smoothing will be enhanced when change agents *acknowledge different worldviews and look for overlap*. A single, "correct" worldview is not necessary to lay this groundwork. Finance, engineering, and ecology may seem worlds apart, but they do share some precepts: for example, diversify the portfolio (preserve nature's gene bank); build in a safety margin (ensure a harvest buffer). Even if a common worldview were desirable, people resist conversion strategies however much they are dressed up to be scientific or educational. To put it in architectural terms, people can disagree vehemently about building design, but they all want solid foundations.

There may also be *leverage at the top*, that is, in finance. No economy can be economical of resources and waste sinks when its financiers are spendthrifts. Finance itself must be grounded, ecologically and socially. There is a Nobel Prize waiting for the person who combines time-honored, prudential financial principles (e.g., spend the interest, not the principal; build only what can be insured) with time-honored ecological and agrarian principles (e.g., don't eat the seed corn; maintain a manageable eyes-to-acres ratio).[12] An economy so structured, from bottom to top and top to bottom, would be grounded in place—a home economy, not a house of cards.

The foundations of this grand industrial edifice, this high-consuming, debt-laden, cost-displacing, fossil-fuel-dependent economy are indeed rocking. Times are changing, fundamentally, like it or not. A new normal is coming, ready or not. What this book does, I hope (and does realistically, I would like to think), is help readers accustomed to easy money and easy goods get ready. Not by changing light bulbs or buying a fuel-efficient car, and certainly not by dialing up the guilt meter. Rather, I hope to have convinced the reader that creating images of the possible and employing language of the ecological and ethical, of good work and sufficient resource use are necessary first steps in laying groundwork for a home economy in an ecological order. The task at hand is living well by living well within our means. It will not be easy or convenient or quick. But with persistence, hard work, and some well-placed interventions, much will be simple and, very likely, rewarding.

Notes

Preface

1. Edward Abbey, *Desert Solitaire: A Season in the Wilderness* (New York: McGraw-Hill, 1968), 126.

Chapter One

1. Quoted in World Wide Fund for Nature (WWF International), Zoological Society of London, and Global Footprint Network, *Living Planet Report 2008* (Gland, Switzerland: WWF, 2008), 1; J. R. McNeill, *Something New Under the Sun: An Environmental History of the Twentieth-Century World* (New York: W. W. Norton, 2000), 48; William J. Cosgrove and Frank R. Rijsberman for the World Water Council, *World Water Vision: Making Water Everybody's Business* (London: Earthscan, 2000), xxi.

Household debt in the United States, measured by the ratio of debt to personal disposable income, increased from 55 percent in 1960 to an all-time high of 133 percent in 2007. Reuven Glick and Kevin J. Lansing, "U.S. Household Deleveraging and Future Consumption Growth," *FRBSF Economic Letter*, no. 2009-16, May 15, 2009, 3 pp. According to the Peter G. Peterson Foundation, U.S. national debt was nearly $11 trillion in 2008, but its current and future financial obligations total $56.4 trillion, or $184,000 for every American. "What Is the Real National Debt?" http://www.pgpf.org/about/nationaldebt (accessed June 1, 2009).

The American Society of Civil Engineers estimates future infrastructure investment costs in the United States to be $2.2 trillion over five years; "2009 Report Card for America's Infrastructure," infrastructurereportcard.org (accessed June 1, 2009).

The end of cheap oil is now widely accepted, whether or not analysts accept the term *peak oil*. See Robert L. Hirsch, "The Inevitable Peaking of World Oil Production," *Atlantic Council Bulletin* 16, no. 3 (October 2005): 1–9; Richard D. Kerr, "World Oil Crunch Looming?" *Science* 322, no. 21 (November 2008): 1178–1179; International Energy Agency, *World Energy Outlook 2008*, http://www.iea.org/weo/2008.asp (accessed May 20, 2009). For historical and future perspectives on fossil fuel see M. King Hubbert, "Exponential Growth as a Transient Phenomenon in Human History," in *Valuing the Earth: Economics, Ecology, Ethics*, ed. Herman E. Daly and Kenneth N. Townsend, 113–126 (Cambridge, MA: MIT Press, 1993); Charles Hall, Pradeep Tharakan, John Hallock, Cutler Cleveland, and Michael Jefferson, "Hydrocarbons and the Evolution of Human Culture," *Nature* 426, no. 20 (November 2003): 318–322; Adam R. Brandt and Alexander E. Farrell, "Scraping the Bottom of the Barrel: Greenhouse Gas Emission Consequences of a Transition to Low-Quality and Synthetic Petroleum Resources," *Climate Change* 84 (2007): 241–263. For a scientific estimate of the great disparities in the distribution of environmental costs and benefits between rich and poor nations, see U. Thara Srinivasan, Susan P. Carey, Eric Hallstein, Paul A. T. Higgins, Amber C. Kerr, Laura E. Koteen, Adam B. Smith, Reg Watson, John Harte, and Richard B. Norgaard, "The Debt of Nations and the Distribution of Ecological Impacts from Human Activities," *PNAS* 2008, National Academy of Sciences of the USA; www.pnas.org/cgi/doi/10.1073/pnas.0709562104 (accessed June 6, 2009).

2. International Energy Agency, *World Energy Outlook 2008*.

3. On material flow and its tight coupling with economic growth, see World Resources Institute, *The Weight of Nations: Material Outflows from Industrial Economies* (Washington, DC: World Resources Institute, 2000).

4. Chap. 10 presents a dramatization of metaphors of the environment. For an explanation of the role of metaphor in science see David E. Leary, "Naming and Knowing: Giving Forms to Things Unknown," *Social Research* 62, no. 2 (summer 1995), 14 pp., proquest.umi.com.proxy.lib.umich.edu. And on military metaphors and their policy implications in global environmental politics, see Maurie J. Cohen, "The 'War' against Global Climate Change and Emergent Debates on Rationing," submitted for publication, New Jersey Institute of Technology, 2009.

Chapter Three

1. Thomas L. Friedman, "The Power of Green: What Does America Need to Regain Its Global Stature?" *New York Times Magazine*, April 15, 2007, 40–51, 67, 71–72 (quotes on 50, 51, 71).

2. For two excellent explorations of this question—what an economy is for—see Gerard Alonzo Smith, "The Purpose of Wealth: A Historical Perspective," in *Valuing the Earth: Economics, Ecology, Ethics*, ed. Herman E. Daly and Kenneth N. Townsend, 183–209 (Cambridge, MA: MIT Press, 1993); Wendell Berry, *Home Economics: Fourteen Essays by Wendell Berry* (San Francisco: North Point Press, 1987).

3. For elaboration of the history and rhetoric of the idea of efficiency, see Thomas Princen, *The Logic of Sufficiency* (Cambridge, MA: MIT Press, 2005), chaps. 3 and 4.

Chapter Four

1. For a riveting account of these early abolitionists, see Adam Hochschild, *Bury the Chains: Prophets and Rebels in the Fight to Free an Empire's Slaves* (Boston: Houghton Mifflin, 2005).

2. James B. Davies, Susanna Sandström, Anthony Shorrocks, and Edward N. Wolff, "The World Distribution of Household Wealth" (discussion paper, United Nations University–World Institute for Development Economics Research, Helsinki, Finland, 2008), http://www.wider.unu.edu/publications/working-papers/discussion-papers/2008/en_GB/dp2008-03 (accessed August 31, 2009).

3. Jared Diamond, "What's Your Consumption Factor?" *New York Times*, January 2, 2008.

4. C. Mandil, "Our Energy for the Future," *S.A.P.I.E.N.S.* 1, no. 1 (2008): 43–44 (quote on 44).

5. Robert Chambers, *Rural Development: Putting the Last First* (New York: Longman Scientific and Technical, 1983), cited in Susanna Hecht and Alexander Cockburn, *The Fate of the Forest: Developers, Destroyers and Defenders of the Amazon* (New York: Harper Perennial, 1990), 228.

6. For the best discussions of the requisite education for a sustainable society, see the work of David Orr: for example, *Ecological Literacy: Education and the Transition to a Postmodern World* (Albany: State University of New York Press, 1992).

Chapter Five

1. For the research behind the principles in this chapter, see the empirical and conceptual work in Thomas Princen, *The Logic of Sufficiency* (Cambridge, MA: MIT Press, 2005), where an account of efficiency's track record, historical, technical, and, most pernicious, political, can be found in chaps. 3 and 4; Thomas Princen, Michael Maniates, and Ken Conca, eds., *Confronting Consumption* (Cambridge, MA: MIT Press, 2002); and Thomas Princen, "Distant Horizons: An Ethic of the Long Term" (in progress).

2. Part of the story of shifting lobster practices can be found in chap. 7 of Princen, *The Logic of Sufficiency*. See also James A. Acheson, *The Lobster Gangs of Maine* (Hanover, NH: University Press of New England, 1988).

Chapter Six

1. Nicholas Georgescu-Roegen, "Selections from 'Energy and Economic Myths,'" in *Valuing the Earth: Economics, Ecology, Ethics*, ed. Herman E. Daly and Kenneth N. Townsend, 89–112 (Cambridge, MA: MIT Press, 1993).

2. James J. Kay, "A Nonequilibrium Thermodynamic Framework for Discussing Ecosystem Integrity," *Environmental Management* 15, no. 4 (1991): 483–495; Gary K. Meffe and C. Ronald Carroll, *Principles of Conservation Biology* (Sunderland, MA: Sinauer, 1994).

Chapter Seven

1. *American Heritage Dictionary of the English Language*, 4th ed. (Boston: Houghton Mifflin, 2000), 566.

2. Michael Ende, *Momo*, trans. J. Maxwell Brownjohn (Garden City, NY: Doubleday, 1985), 28–29.

3. Wendell Berry, *Home Economics: Fourteen Essays by Wendell Berry* (San Francisco: North Point Press, 1987), 145.

4. Why a thought experiment? It's unlikely that any reader (let alone this author) is going to build an entire economy, an economical, ecological, sustaining economy, a "home economy." But it is very likely that every reader will be making some tough choices in the coming years, some brought on by conventional economic failures (if finan-

cial derivatives, global capital flows, and government bailouts in the billions and trillions of dollars can be considered "conventional") and some by biophysical realities (for instance, pandemic disease, prolonged water shortage, severe storms, and the end of cheap oil). Each of these choices will be shaped by rules of thumb, guiding principles. Unfortunately, the guidance that people have today is "Buy green, click to show support, email your congressperson, and write a check" (see the multimillion-dollar campaign at wecansolveit.org for an illustration). So the point of the thought experiment is to begin to imagine an alternative economy, a necessary step in actually enacting an alternative economy.

5. Christopher Lasch, *The True and Only Heaven: Progress and Its Critics* (New York: W. W. Norton, 1991), 204.

6. On ecological distancing, see Thomas Princen, "Distancing: Consumption and the Severing of Feedback," in *Confronting Consumption*, ed. Thomas Princen, Michael Maniates, and Ken Conca, 103–131 (Cambridge, MA: MIT Press, 2002).

Chapter Eight

1. Ford Motor Company advertisement with Kermit the Frog and the Ford Escape Hybrid, video.google.com/videoplay?doc id=7372950930856015507 (accessed November 17, 2008).

2. The following is an abridged version of Thomas Princen, "Consumer Sovereignty, Heroic Sacrifice: Two Insidious Concepts in an Endlessly Expansionist Economy," in *The Environmental Politics of Sacrifice*, ed. Michael Maniates and John Meyer (Cambridge, MA: MIT Press, forthcoming).

3. With the global financial crisis and forced economic contraction beginning in 2008, the framing of this consumption conundrum might be somewhat different, but the thrust is the same. Economy saviors say: We must stimulate the economy, get people to spend more. We can get back to saving the environment after we save the economy, which is to say, after society returns to its high-consuming, debt-laden, cost-deferring ways.

4. Institutes of Health report cited in Paul Krugman, "Death by Insurance," *New York Times*, May 1, 2006.

5. I thank sociologist Michael Bell for making this important distinction.

6. I thank psychologist Raymond De Young for raising this point.

7. I thank resource analyst Jack Manno for pointing out the absence of commitment and the depreciation of relations (with others and the natural world) in a commoditized, consumer economy. Personal communication, May 23, 2006. See also Manno's "Commoditization: Consumption Efficiency and an Economy of Care and Connection," in *Confronting Consumption*, ed. Thomas Princen, Michael Maniates, and Ken Conca, 67-99 (Cambridge, MA: MIT Press, 2002).

8. Karen Litfin, "The Sacred and the Profane in the Politics of Sacrifice," in Maniates and Meyer, *The Environmental Politics of Sacrifice* (forthcoming).

9. Ibid.

10. William Leach, *Land of Desire: Merchants, Power, and the Rise of a New American Culture* (New York: Vintage, 1993).

11. I have to admit that, at times, walking to work does feel like sacrifice in the negative sense: near-collisions with careless drivers throw some doubt on whether all these benefits exceed the risks to life and limb.

Chapter Nine

1. Christopher Lasch, *The True and Only Heaven: Progress and Its Critics* (New York: W. W. Norton, 1991), 184–225.

2. This chapter is adapted from a longer and more historically detailed piece, "Enough Work, Enough Consumption," chap. 5 of *The Logic of Sufficiency* (Cambridge, MA: MIT Press, 2005).

3. The admittedly awkward term *producerist* reflects the fact that our language lacks a term for "worker" that implies self-direction, dignity, and creativity. Some readers may prefer to substitute *artisan, craftsman, freelancer, tinker,* or *wright*.

4. For vivid accounts of the expansionist, progressive ideal in the American Midwest, see William Cronon, *Nature's Metropolis: Chicago and the Great West* (New York: W. W. Norton, 1991); and in the arid American West, see Donald Worster, *Rivers of Empire: Water, Aridity, and the Growth of the American West* (New York: Oxford University Press, 1985).

5. Lasch, *True and Only Heaven*, 204.

6. Ibid., 211.

7. It might be surmised that the producerist ideal was a thing of the past, totally eclipsed by the progressive consensus, as Lasch seems

to suggest. But I submit that it is alive and well, albeit nearly invisible in mainstream popular culture. Small proprietors still, I believe, outnumber executives and organized labor. And independent farmers still survive despite the aggressions of agribusiness and government agencies.

8. Michael Ende, *Momo*, translated by J. Maxwell Brownjohn (Garden City, NY: Doubleday, 1985), 29.

9. Lasch, *True and Only Heaven*, 531.

10. Dr. Seuss (Theodore Seuss Geisel), *The Lorax* (New York: Random House, 1971), no page numbers.

11. Personal communication, Raymond De Young, 2003. See also Steven Kaplan, "The Restorative Benefits of Nature: Toward an Integrative Framework," *Journal of Environmental Psychology* 15 (1995): 169–182.

12. *The Lord of the Rings: The Fellowship of the Ring* (2001), http://www.imdb.com/title/tt0120737/quotes (accessed June 10, 2009).

13. Melvin L. Kohn, "Unresolved Issues in the Relationship between Work and Personality," in *The Nature of Work: Sociological Perspectives*, ed. Kai Erikson and Steven Peter Vallas (New Haven, CT: Yale University Press, 1990), 36–68, 41–42; emphasis added.

14. Wendell Berry, "Discipline and Hope," in *A Continuous Harmony: Essays Cultural and Agricultural* (New York: Harcourt Brace Jovanovich, 1972); reprinted in Berry, *Recollected Essays, 1965–1980*, 151–220 (New York: North Point Press, 1998), 220.

Chapter Ten

1. Erazim Kohák, "Of Dwelling and Wayfaring: A Quest for Metaphors," in *The Longing for Home*, ed. Leroy S. Rouner, 30–46 (Notre Dame, IN: Notre Dame University Press, 1976), 31.

2. George Lakoff and Mark Johnson, *Metaphors We Live By* (Chicago: University of Chicago Press, 1980), 145–146.

Chapter Eleven

1. I thank Paul Princen for suggesting this term.

2. While I speak here about direct experience, much learning also occurs indirectly, through story and picture and dance, say, or a good

movie and a video game. These too can lead to new worldviews. Raymond De Young, 2008, personal communication.

3. William James, *The Principles of Psychology* (New York: Holt, 1890), 1:424.

4. I thank psychologists Raymond De Young and Tim Kasser for working through this section.

5. I am obviously only selecting a portion of the financial world, what might be better termed "classic finance," that which has ancient roots— insuring, saving, investing, diversifying.

6. J. H. Barkow, Leda Cosmides, and John Tooby, eds., *The Adapted Mind: Evolutionary Psychology and the Generation of Culture* (New York: Oxford University Press, 1992); David J. Buller, *Adapting Minds: Evolutionary Psychology and the Persistent Quest for Human Nature* (Cambridge, MA: MIT Press, 2005).

Chapter Twelve

1. Howard Markel, MD, "Tracing the Cigarette's Path from Sexy to Deadly," *New York Times*, March 20, 2007.

2. Allan M. Brandt, *The Cigarette Century: The Rise, Fall and Deadly Persistence of the Product That Defined America* (New York: Basic Books, 2007), 497.

3. Ibid., 13; Duff Wilson, "Regulating Tobacco Industry Is a Recent Concept," *New York Times*, June 12, 2009.

4. Markel, "Tracing the Cigarette's Path."

5. There are great uncertainties regarding fossil-fuel reserves. Estimates range from some four or five times what humans have already burned to nearly twenty times. Adam R. Brandt and Alexander E. Farrell, "Scraping the Bottom of the Barrel: Greenhouse Gas Emission Consequences of a Transition to Low-Quality and Synthetic Petroleum Resources," *Climate Change* 84 (2007): 241–263.

6. This is a near-verbatim rant I overheard in my place of employment, the School of Natural Resources and Environment at the University of Michigan. Sadly, variations of such language are not that uncommon among committed environmentalists.

7. Michael Maniates, "Going Green? Easy Doesn't Do It," *Washington Post*, November 22, 2007.

8. I thank Maurie Cohen for bringing this point to my attention.

9. Herman E. Daly, *Beyond Growth: The Economics of Sustainable Development* (Boston: Beacon Press, 1996).

10. Thomas Pynchon, *Gravity's Rainbow* (New York: Penguin, 2000), 251; cited on p. 159 in William R. Freudenburg and Margarita Alario, "Weapons of Mass Distraction: Magicianship, Misdirection, and the Dark Side of Legitimation," *Sociological Forum* 22, no. 2 (June 2007): 146–173.

11. Or, as one certified member of the upcoming generation put it in reviewing the manuscript for this book, it's time for the older generation to step aside. Personal communication, Maria Princen, June 7, 2009.

12. Modern agrarians Wendell Berry and Wes Jackson argue that when a farmer's acreage gets too large, beyond one's capacity to directly monitor the soil and water and grasses, external inputs such as pesticides and fertilizers become necessary, along with all the attendant problems of land degradation and farm debt. See "A Defense of the Family Farm," in Wendell Berry, *Home Economics: Fourteen Essays by Wendell Berry* (San Francisco: North Point Press, 1987), 164.

Index

Abbey, Edward (writer), on water, vii, 77, 188
Adapting mind, 175–176
Adaptive strategy, 160, 164, 171–172
Artisan, 99, 121–122, 202n3. *See also* Work

Berry, Wendell (agrarian, social critic), 77, 96–97, 205n13
Brandt, Allan M. (medical historian), on smoking, 181
Burden of proof, 33, 55, 114

Chambers, Robert (international development specialist), on political will, 54–55
Confidence, 10–11, 23, 43, 151
in financial system, 22, 42, 52, 102, 171
Consumer sovereignty, 43–45, 98, 108–109, 114, 116, 123. *See also* Demand
Consumption, 12, 42, 53, 55, 116, 130, 183
and ecological capital, 1, 125
in an economical economy, 95
economy's dependency on, 44, 98, 106–107, 201n3

and growth, 30–39, 47, 82, 124
Consumerism, 83, 94, 113, 122
Crisis
and behavior change, 50–53, 173, 185 (*see also* Social change)
global, 2, 201n3
material, 3–4, 6

Daly, Herman E. (ecological economist), 191
Demand. *See also* Consumer sovereignty; Consumption; Discipline
consumer, 9, 10, 21, 44, 45, 114, 123
of leaders, 77, 175
from nature, 5, 71, 85, 124
from needy, 71
De Young, Raymond (environmental psychologist), ix, xi, 128
Discipline, 22, 95–97, 124. *See also* Ethic; Work
Diversion. *See* Framing

Ecological integrity, 88, 150–151, 154

Ecological order, 2, 16–18, 63–
64, 69, 74, 75, 116–117. *See
also* Industrial order
adaptiveness in, 164
metaphors for, 154
value in, 86–89
work in, 120–127
and worldview, 171, 174, 190
Economy. *See also* Consumer
sovereignty; Demand; Home
economy
care in an, 71, 95
consumer, 38, 107, 116, 201n3
economical, 2–3, 23, 71, 91–
92, 95, 97, 120
mature versus immature, 70–71
of nature, 34–35, 97
the one and only, 23, 29–32,
35, 38
of practice, 63, 133–134
producer, 97–102
sustainable, 33, 36, 43, 61,
68–69, 76, 162
Efficiency, 45–47, 54, 67–68,
114, 121, 191
Ende, Michael (children's author), 96
Environmentalism, 11, 159,
204n6
Ethic, 5, 14, 17–18, 91–92, 101–
102, 195. *See also* Normative
of the citizen, 125
consumer, 44, 94, 112, 114,
116
of the industrial order, 2–3
of the long term, 58, 192–193
in worldviews, 62
Excess, 12, 69, 82–83, 106,
187–188, 191–192. *See also*
Sufficiency
of an economy, vii, 17, 68, 98,
108

and sufficiency, 74
Externality, 41–42, 114

Foundations, 4, 9–11, 17, 22–
23, 49, 77, 125, 151, 194.
See also Fundamental shift;
Grounding
Framing, 17–18, 102, 167,
201n3
diversionary, 47, 54, 114, 191
as optimal depletion, 92–93
of sacrifice, 107–109, 113
as tool for social change, 120,
177, 191
Fundamental shift, 5–9, 53, 75,
173, 176, 179, 183–185,
189–190. *See also* Foundations; Normative

Gloom and doom, viii–x, 11, 58,
105, 179–180, 185
Growth, 10, 120–121, 173, 185.
See also Consumption; Language; Metaphor
in consumption, 32–33, 42–43
economic, 1, 3, 8, 33, 41, 68,
93–94, 190–191
material, 33, 82–83
nonmaterial, 159
Grounding. *See also*
Foundations
ecological, 2, 3–5, 17, 24, 35,
74, 150, 193–195
metaphorical, 12–13, 154
moral, 10–12
in place, 124, 133–134, 186,
190
of worldviews, 169

Home economy, 3, 17, 24, 27,
38, 58, 95–97, 155, 162,
200–201n4

principles for, 64, 69–77, 91–92, 194
work in, 127
Hopefulness, ix, x, 5, 18, 57, 101–102, 184
sinks for, 185–187
sources for, 187–194

Industrial order, 117, 122, 131, 157–158. *See also* Ecological order

James, William (psychologist, philosopher), 161
Johnson, Mark (linguistic philosopher), 153–154

Kohak, Erazim (philosopher), 153
Kohn, Melvin (social psychologist), 130

Lakoff, George (cognitive linguist), 153–154
Language, x, 12–13, 17, 135, 153–154, 157. *See also* Metaphor; Reconnection
of connection, 84
of the economy, 35–36, 157, 185
of new normal, 193
of smoking, 182
of value, 85
Lasch, Christopher (historian, social critic), 99, 120, 121, 122, 124
Limits, 18, 52–53, 64, 74–77, 124–128, 171
in work, 119, 128–129, 131–134
Litfin, Karen (political theorist), on sacrifice, 112, 113

Long term, 17, 64, 85, 89, 117, 123–124, 189–190, 193. *See also* Ethic; Time
the ecological, 74–75, 88, 102
worldviews and, 162, 166, 171

Maniates, Michael (political scientist), on consumer choice, xi, 186–187
Markel, Howard (medical historian), on smoking, 180–181, 182
Meadows, Donella (systems analyst), 106
Metaphor, 18, 40, 70, 150, 153–154, 155, 191, 193. *See also* Language
from natural systems, 12–13, 36, 72, 85, 171
Metrics, 97, 192

Normal, new versus old, vii, xi, 9–13, 18, 31, 70, 182–184, 185, 193–194
historical shifts and, 50–52, 158, 180–182
Normative, 14, 53, 67, 154, 163, 192–193. *See also* Ecological integrity; Ethic; Value

Optimal depletion, 92–94

Patten, Simon (economist), on consumption, 124–125
Peak oil, 7, 198n1
Pluralism, 18, 84, 160, 171
Political will, 53–55, 108
Principles, social organizing, 58, 64, 67, 92, 154, 170, 192, 200n1. *See also* Ethic; Home economy; Normative; Prudence

Principles (cont.)
  capping, 74–75
  and consumerism, 125–126
  of finance and ecology, 170, 194
  intermittency, 69–71
  source, 76–77
  sufficiency, 72–74
  of sustainable use, 37, 69, 101
Problem solving, ix, 175, 184
Progress, 16, 27, 30, 120–121, 124–125. *See also* Growth
  and material abundance, 40–41, 85
Prudence, 92, 101, 113, 194

Reconnection, 82–87, 126
Restraint, 16, 63–64, 73, 76–77, 132, 155, 158
  and consumerism, 125
Risk, 3, 10, 12, 18, 101, 144–145, 184, 190

Sacrifice, 55
  positive versus negative, 71, 74, 89, 106–117
  and the sacred, 76–77
Slavery, as analog, 50–52, 183
Smoking, as analog, 194–199
Social change, 50, 158. *See also* Crisis; Framing
  theory of, 185–186, 190–191
Social order. *See* Ecological order; Industrial order
Sufficiency, 25, 34, 72–74, 108, 171, 191, 195. *See also* Excess; Principles
Sustainability, 162, 168–172, 174, 187–188. *See also* Ecological order; Economy

Throughput, 33, 75, 82–83, 98
Time, 163, 165, 193. *See also* Long term; Work
  ecological, 10, 17, 89–90, 102
  natural, 126–127
  task-based, 96, 129–131

Value
  commercial, 90, 95, 107, 110–111, 137, 192
  in ecological order, 17, 84, 85–90
  of a resource, 88
  in work, 79, 87

Work, 90, 119–120. *See also* Artisan; Discipline; Ecological order; Limits; Reconnection; Time; Value
  good, x, 24, 79, 85, 96–98, 101, 117
  self-direction in, 122, 131, 202n3
Worldview, x, 18, 135, 153, 157, 159, 190, 194, 203–204n2
  as adaptation, 167–172, 175–177
  agrarian, 166
  economistic, 167
  of the environment, 160–164
  mechanistic, 165–166
  naturist, 165